# Supporting Speech, Language and Communication Needs

# Supporting Speech, Language and Communication Needs

## Working with students aged 11 to 19

Kate Ripley and Jenny Barrett

Los Angeles • London • New Delhi • Singapore • Washington DC

SAGE Publications Ltd
1 Oliver's Yard
55 City Road
London EC1Y 1SP

SAGE Publications Inc.
2455 Teller Road
Thousand Oaks, California 91320

SAGE Publications India Pvt Ltd
B 1/I 1 Mohan Cooperative Industrial Area
Mathura Road
New Delhi 110 044

SAGE Publications Asia-Pacific Pte Ltd
33 Pekin Street #02-01
Far East Square
Singapore 048763

**Library of Congress Control Number: 2007936858**

**British Library Cataloguing
in Publication data**

A catalogue record for this book is available from the British Library

ISBN 978-1-4129-4760-2
ISBN 978-1-4129-4761-9 (pbk)

Typeset by CEPHA Imaging Pvt. Ltd., Bangalore, India
Printed in Great Britain by The Cromwell Press Ltd, Trowbridge, Wiltshire.

# Contents

# Downloadable Materials

Wherever you see the ⌖ icon then a downloadable materials can be found at HYPERLINK "http://www.sagepub.co.uk/sutherland" http://www.sagepub.co.uk/ripley for use in your setting. For a full list please see below.

## Chapter 2 – Understanding Comprehension
2.1  IEP Master Proforma
2.2  Comprehension Monitoring
2.3  Tourism & Leisure
2.4  Language Advice and General Strategies
2.5  Templates for Flow Charts
2.6  Key Wording of a Neurological Text
2.7  Simple text to Discuss Inference 1
2.8  Units of Measurement: Baseline Assessment
2.9  Daily Lesson Plan: Time Concepts/Comp Monitoring

## Chapter 3 – Remembering Memory
3.1  Templates For Flow Charts

## Chapter 6 – Talking Language
6.1  Small Group Work – Vocabulary Learning and Retrieval

## Chapter 7 – Socially Speaking
7.1  Social Skills Practice Pack
7.2  Session Plans for Social Skills Groups
7.3  A Sample Session Plan – Asking and Responding to Questions

## Chapter 8 – Talking Behaviour
8.1  Proforma Narrative Analysis

## Chapter 9 – Assessing Speech and Language
9.1  Identifying Students Who Have Speech and Language Impairments in the Secondary Classroom
9.2  Speech and Language Checklist
9.3  Structured Observation
9.4  Observation Checklist

## Chapter 10 – Parents Talking
10.1 Interview Questionnaire

## Appendix
Figure 2.5
Figure 2.7

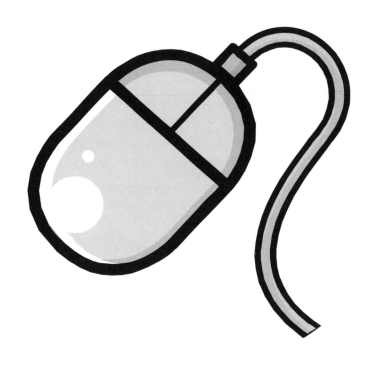

# Acknowledgements

Grateful thanks to all those who have contributed to the book, through their advice, comments and allowing us to reproduce lesson plans.

- Louise Andrews – speech and language therapist, the Swan Centre, Falmer School, Brighton
- Anne Clarke – specialist teacher for speech and language impairment, Brighton
- Sue Mildinhall, head speech and language therapist, South Thames Cleft Service, Guy's Hospital, London
- Hilary Dumbrill, specialist speech and language therapist, Hamilton Lodge School for Children with Deafness, Brighton
- Parents who participated in the interview questionnaire for the final chapter of the book.
- Viv Hughes, senior educational psychologist, East Sussex.

As always, our profound gratitude to Tracy who has endeavoured to control our literacy excesses and produced a manuscript with perfect clarity. Also special thanks for her unfailing patience and good humour!

# About the Authors

**Kate Ripley** BA (Leeds), BA (London), PGCE, MsE, is a senior specialist educational psychologist working in Hampshire. Kate was head of department in a secondary school when she left teaching to raise children and train as an educational psychologist. She subsequently worked as an educational psychologist with specialist language schools (Invalid Children's Aid Nationwide) and for local authorities as a specialist psychologist, assistant principal educational psychologist and acting principal psychologist. Kate is a regional tutor for Birmingham University, Speech, Language and Communication Needs course and president of the National Association of Professionals Concerned with Language Impaired Children (NAPLIC). Her current research interest is the link between language impairment and social, emotional and behavioural difficulties.

Kate is also a regular contributor to national and international conferences and training courses with a focus on speech, language and communication needs. Recent publications include: *Dyspraxia: A Guide for Parents & Teachers* (1998) with Bob Daines and Jenny Barrett; *Inclusion of Children with Dyspraxia/DCD: A Handbook for Teachers* (2001); *Inclusion of Children with Speech and Language Impairments: Accessing the Curriculum and Promoting Personal and Social Development* (2001) with Pam Fleming and Jenny Barrett; and *First Steps to Emotional Literacy* (2007) with Elspeth Simpson.

**Jenny Barrett** MA, MRCSLT Cert Ed, is qualified both as a speech and language therapist and a teacher, and has been working on a consultancy basis since retiring from her post of chief of services for education with her employer South Downs Health (NHS) Trust (now Children and Young People's Trust) in Brighton, East Sussex. Her long and varied career has taken her from the East End of London to the Rocky Mountains of Canada, where she worked on a multidisciplinary research project testing the feasibility of integrating children with physical disability into mainstream education.

Her main areas of interest during the past 20 years have been with specific language impairment (SLI), and communication of the needs of children with this condition to colleagues, other professionals and parents. She has participated in various research projects on the subject of SLI and lectures nationally with her colleague Kate Ripley on the subject of dyspraxia/ developmental co-ordination disorder (DCD). Jenny has authored and co-authored three books: *Help Me Speak – A Parents Guide to Speech and Language Therapy* (1994); *Dyspraxia: A Guide for Parents & Teachers* (1998) with Bob Daines and Kate Ripley; and *Inclusion of Children with Speech and Language Impairments: Accessing the Curriculum and Promoting Personal and Social Development* (2001) with Pam Fleming and Kate Ripley.

# How to Use this book

In this book we aim to:

- explain the range of SLCN which may be experienced by students in key stages 3 and 4
- help SENCOs, teachers to identify the SLCN of students
- explore practical ways to support these students in the classroom context
- present a range of strategies that might be used with individual students or small groups of students
- explore the implications for social inclusion and address social, emotional and behavioural issues.

Chapters 2 to 7, which focus on the different aspects of SLCN, have a similar framework which includes:

- quotes from teachers when they are describing the problems that students appear to experience in their classes
- quotes from students when they attempt to describe their problems from their own perspective
- case study examples of students who have experienced the particular SLCN which is the focus of the chapter.

These sections will help to sensitise a SENCO, or other staff, as to which aspect(s) of language the student may be struggling with.

Each area of language is described and practical ideas to support the students are set out. These will include whole class strategies to share with subject teachers and specific intervention strategies that might be used by support staff.

Some terms in this book refer to practices in England, Wales and Northern Ireland (e.g. OFSTED, key stage 3). For a full explanation of these terms, including the age ranges the various key stages cover, please see Appendix I.

# 1

# Speech, Language and Communication Impairment Explained

**Chapter Objectives**

> To set out the aims and framework of the book
> To explore different ways of describing language
> To identify the key components of effective communication
> To provide a framework for understanding language development
> To explore the implications of the interaction between language development and language demands in key stage 3 and key stage 4

## 1.1 Introduction

Difficulties with speech and language are most closely associated with the early years, so it is easy to assume that students at secondary school or college are able to understand and use language in order to learn. However, this assumption cannot be made for students who have a history of speech, language and communication needs (SLCN) or others who may experience more general learning difficulties.

By the time children with a history of SLCN start the secondary phase of their education any persisting difficulties may be quite difficult to identify. The obvious signs, primarily difficulties with speech, have usually been resolved unless there is a physical cause; for example, cerebral palsy. We are able to understand what they are saying and make the assumption that they are able to understand what we are saying. We also assume that they are able to express their needs, wishes and feelings, if they choose to do so.

The optimistic view that language problems are an issue primarily for the early years was challenged by a national longitudinal study of children with SLCN (Conti-Ramsden and Botting, 1999) which reported that in year 2 only 1% of the estimated 5% of children with specific language impairment had been identified on the special needs registers in school. Four percent of children with SLCN did not have their primary need identified in key stage 1. Children who were the most likely to have had their difficulties identified in their early years and may have had speech and language therapy (SLT) were those who had problems with speech production usually associated either with limited control of the articulatory system or problems with their sound system (phonology). Many of these children would have been discharged from SLT before starting school because their speech was intelligible.

Children with SLCN had often been given a range of other labels or had individual education plans that focused on the secondary effects of their core language problem. Common examples included:

- Dyslexia – when they were slow to learn to read and spell because of the effect of residual problems with their sound system (phonological system) on their ability to access the phonic route to reading.
- Social, emotional, behavioural difficulties (SEBD) – because of the impact that a language impairment may have on social, emotional and behavioural development.
- Autistic spectrum condition (ASC, also known as ASD) – because of the impact that a language impairment may have on patterns of social interaction and social communication. Typically, as the language of these children improves, the early 'autistic-type' features recede.

Some children with SLCN who were in the 'missing' 4% at key stage 1 may be identified during key stage 2. The two most common markers are: when the children find it hard to access the more demanding language of instruction, or when their decoding skills for reading are found to be in advance of their reading comprehension (Snowling and Stackhouse, 1996). However, there are students who have primary language needs who may transfer to secondary school without their core language difficulties having been identified.

Andy and Alice are typical examples of children whose language needs were not addressed before they started at secondary school.

 Case study: Andy

Andy had a history of behavioural difficulties at school and the Behavioural Support Services has worked with him, his family and the school.

He was referred to the Speech and Language Therapy Service while at infant school but he has refused to co-operate with the assessment.

Andy was included in a transition group in year 6 which met at the local secondary school. He was assessed in school by the educational psychologist during the autumn term year 7:

- Non-verbal abilities – average range
- Receptive language – low average, except semantic knowledge first centile (i.e. 99% of students of his age would be expected to obtain a higher score)
- Expressive language – first centile
- A reluctant communicator – speech not fully intelligible
- Low tolerance of failure when tasks become challenging
- Low self-esteem as a learner – 'I'm think'

Andy's behaviour in school was challenging:

- Confrontational and abusive to staff
- Volatile and aggressive to other students
- Refusal to attempt classroom tasks
- Refusal to do homework

 Case study: Alice

Alice attended a mainstream school, moved schools at the time of family breakdown and returned to her first school from year 3 onwards.

Staff at the junior school had no significant concerns about her educational progress or social development, so she was not on the SEN register.

Alice transferred to secondary school having attained levels 3/4 for key stage 2 SATs. In year 9 Alice became increasingly reluctant to attend school.

Assessment by an educational psychologist revealed:

- Verbal skills at 0.3 centile; that is, 99% of students her age would be expected to obtain a higher score
- Social communication skills were an area of relative strength so that she was able to:
  - take turns in conversation
  - initiate and close a conversational exchange skillfully
  - adapt what she said to the needs of the listener
  - demonstrate appropriate prosody and non-verbal communication skills

Alice's relatively strong social skills and social communication skills, together with her age-appropriate decoding skills for reading and encoding for spelling appear to have masked her significant, core difficulties with language comprehension until her inability to access the year 9 curriculum led to school refusal.

## 1.2 Describing language

> Children who are unable to communicate effectively through language, or to use language as a basis for further learning, are handicapped socially, educationally and, as a consequence emotionally. Byers-Brown and Edwards (1989)

It is important for teachers who work with students who have SLCN to be familiar with some of the ways that language is described by other professionals. How language is described often depends on the focus of the describer. Thus, speech and language therapists may find that the analysis of a language profile using a psycholinguistic model (Stackhouse and Wells, 1997) helps to guide the planning of a programme of intervention, while a teacher might find a social interactionist model (Barthorpe and Visser, 1991) a more appropriate way of looking at the needs of a student. The form/content/use model (Lahey and Bloom, 1988) is the preferred model for many CPD courses for teachers (described in Ripley *et al.*, 2001). The many ways of describing language reflect the complexity of language as a system in which different aspects and different levels interact. This section introduces some key terminology that is in common use.

### 1.2.1 Language delay and language disorder

Every child learns language in their own way. In some cases children show an unusual delay in the development of their understanding of language and/or their ability to express themselves. Difficulties in these areas will inevitably have some impact on the way in which that child uses language in order to communicate. Fortunately, most children with a language delay do 'catch up', often before they reach school age. For other children, their language develops in an idiosyncratic way. These individuals are described as having a language disorder and their difficulties may persist into key stage 3 or 4. The language problems may affect their access to the curriculum, as well as their social, emotional and behavioural development.

### 1.2.2 Effective communication

In order to communicate effectively we need to be able to listen and understand what is said to us: **receptive language**. There are many subskills which are needed in order to do this, even if we can hear what is said. These skills are described in detail in Chapter 2. We also need to be able to articulate our thoughts, feelings and needs: **expressive language**. This is another complex process which is discussed in Chapter 6.

Some students have adequate levels of receptive and expressive language, but experience communication problems associated with how they use their language. This area of difficulty, known as **pragmatics**, is often the core problem for students on the autistic spectrum. However, students who have difficulties with speech, receptive or expressive language may show secondary problems with the pragmatic aspects of language which recede as their language improves.

The pragmatic aspects of language include the two main components:

- the functions and purposes for which the student uses language
- the way in which the student uses their language (e.g. how they adapt what they say to the 'audience').

Pragmatic skills are discussed in Chapter 7. A glossary of terms is presented in Appendix I. It is possible to illustrate the processes involved in effective communication using a basic input/output model (Figures 1.1 and 1.2).

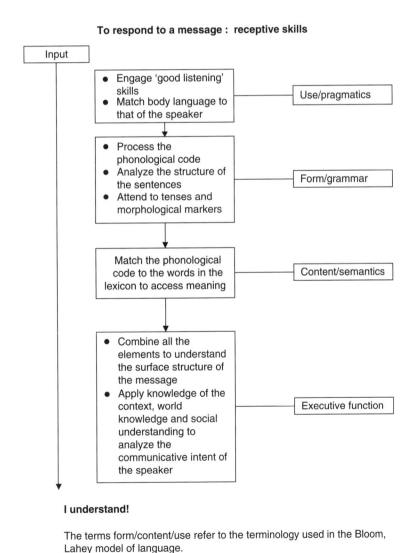

The terms form/content/use refer to the terminology used in the Bloom, Lahey model of language.

**Figure 1.1**  Input/output model.

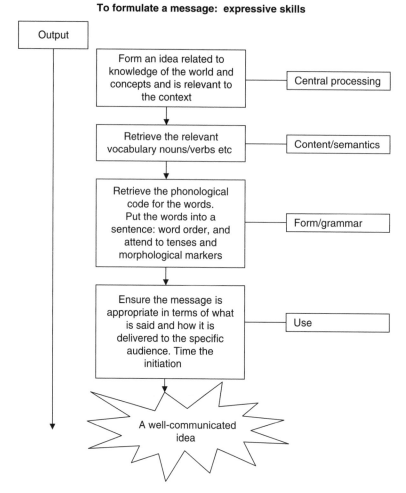

**Figure 1.2** Input/output model.

## 1.3 Language development

For most children, language acquisition is a robust process but for children with SLCN things do not go according to plan. Normal language development follows a biologically ordered schedule and children everywhere follow a similar pattern of development. It is an example of what is known as 'maturationally controlled behaviour'. There is a growing body of evidence, which indicates that SLCN occurs when key gene sequences on chromosomes 16 and 19 have mutated. These different sequences are mostly inherited but new mutations may occur spontaneously. Readers interested in the genetic background to SLCN are referred to the work of Professor Monaco of the Welcome Centre for Human Genetics.

The brains of human babies appear to be pre-programmed to listen to the sounds of language and to interact with their carers. The evidence suggests that babies are able to hear sounds while they are in the womb. They will react to the sound of their mother's voice and other sounds that they have heard, often pre-natally – the Australian research showed recognition of the 'Neighbours' theme tune in the first few days post-natally. Babies quickly learn that some sound patterns recur and these patterns are stored in the part of the brain that stores the memory for sounds (phonological memory).

With the help of their carers (joint attention is involved here) the children learn to attach meaning to these phonological patterns in the phonological memory. The meanings are stored in the part of the brain that stores the memory for word meanings (the lexicon). Children probably recognize about 100 words before they start to say words.

The skills of interaction with carers can be demonstrated at 2-hour old when babies will imitate and take turns in non-verbal conversations (proto conversations). They look intently at the carer's face and by 6 months normally developing babies will follow the direction of the carer's gaze.

Language development is facilitated when the adult names the object they are looking at. Babies also use eye pointing to direct the adult's attention to objects that the adult will usually, obligingly, name. Children on the autistic spectrum do not easily develop this type of joint referencing and may be slower to develop these early naming skills.

At about 18 months babies realize that things have names and can be labelled. They gradually develop the culturally shared knowledge of what a word 'means' – they establish semantic boundaries for words so, for example, they learn that not all men in uniform are firemen, an example of over-extended semantic boundaries. Early semantic boundaries may also be too restricted, for example, 'duck' is the yellow plastic duck in the bath – nothing else.

This process of developing semantic boundaries continues throughout life, and some students entering secondary school may still not have very well-defined semantic boundaries. This may lead to confusions when they are trying to understand the formal, precise language that is used in explanations or instructions in the classroom.

Once children have acquired a critical mass of words they start to combine words. At first they use two-word phrases but eventually grammatically correct sentences are mastered. However, students who have difficulties with grammar may still not use or understand complex sentences with subordinate clauses and may continue to have problems with features such as verb tenses, irregular plural forms or connectors at secondary school. This may not be apparent in their social conversations as these will usually be kept quite simple and take place in a shared, immediate context.

### 1.3.1 Language development and language demands

Children learn their early language skills by interacting with other people and using the language that they need in order to describe objects or actions, to ask for what they want and for a range of other functions which relate to real life demands. The majority of children will be able to use these basic interpersonal communication skills (BICS) by the time they start key stage 3, although normally developing children are in command of social language skills by the end of key stage 1.

When children enter school, or even pre-school, the rules for interaction begin to change. The rules for exchanges are different and words need to take on more precise meanings. They are expected to listen and to understand language that is no longer embedded in the context of everyday actions and a familiar routine. They are also expected to use language to talk about events and things that exist outside the immediate context of the interaction. This more abstract, decontextualized language is the main medium for teaching and learning by the time children enter key stage 3. The ability to access this more complex language has been called 'cognitive academic language proficiency' (CALP) and was first described by Cummins (1986). Cognitive academic language processing continues to develop through the years in formal education and most children gradually improve their skills in interaction with the demands that are made in the classroom throughout key stages 1 and 2. However, in every year 7 group there will be a significant number of children, including those who have a history of SLCN, who find it hard to understand and use abstract, decontextualized language.

While children move from BICS to CALP they begin to develop a conscious awareness of language. They can reflect on language and consciously manipulate the rules of the language system. Puns become a great favourite at this stage of development and they will start to be able to self-correct errors of word selection or grammar. They begin to use abstract language to explain ideas and define words. Before this stage children will often give concrete, anecdotal explanations when asked what words such as 'brave' mean.

- 'When I fell over and don't cry ... Dad said I brave.' (BICS)
- 'When you do something even if it is dangerous or you're frightened.' (CALP)

Once students have acquired the skills of CALP, language is internalized as a tool for thinking. They can begin to plan, hypothesize, explain ideas, engage in verbal reasoning, reflect on imaginary events, understand rules to guide their behaviour, debate and negotiate. All these higher-level functions are needed for academic and social success in secondary school.

## Points to remember

- Language skills are key to learning and social inclusion.
- Some children and students with SLCN do not have their language needs identified in key stage 1 and key stage 2 but persisting unrecognized language problems may become apparent as they attempt to access the secondary curriculum.
- The components of effective communication are receptive language, expressive language and how we use our language: pragmatics.
- How normally developing children acquire language.
- The difference between the language used for social interaction and the meta-linguistic skills that are needed to access the curriculum.

# 2

# Understanding Comprehension

**Chapter Objectives**

> To outline the behavioural signs that may be associated with difficulties of comprehension (receptive language)
> To present the range of skills that is involved in the understanding of spoken and written language
> To identify the specific difficulties that students may have with comprehension
> To provide ideas about how to support students with comprehension difficulties in the mainstream classroom
> To provide ideas about how to support individual students with specific areas of difficulty

In the introduction it was explained how some students who are comfortable using social language, which is needed in order to chat with their friends or answer simple, factual questions, may nevertheless not have mastered the more abstract, decontextualized language code that is required in order to access the language of instruction and explanation which is used in the key stage 3 classroom and beyond. Complex language structures with subordinate clauses may be used in routine instructions such as 'If you have finished the diagram but not the writing, you will need to copy the questions for homework.'

Even at an early age children who find it hard to understand what is said to them start to 'tune' out when they hear complex language and may even start to avoid situations if they think they won't understand (and look silly) or when extended listening is involved.

For Brenda her avoidance strategies were interpreted as surly behaviour. By the time such students enter secondary school they may have developed strong, entrenched patterns of avoidance habits which are often interpreted as behaviour problems because of the ways that they impact on others in the class. Alice (Chapter 1) chatted to friends when she was not listening because she had 'tuned out'. She also got into trouble for talking out of turn when she asked her friends to explain what to do, rather than ask her teachers.

 **Case study: Brenda, Year 10**

Brenda had several changes of primary school. She was bullied at her first secondary school and transferred to a new school in year 9.

She was referred to the Educational Psychology Service at the start of year 10 because of concerns that she might need special arrangements at GCSE because of literacy problems. Brenda was described by some staff as a 'bit sulky' but her social communication skills were not a problem in situations when she felt confident as she had a circle of good friends, including a boyfriend.

Brenda did have recognized strengths in the areas of art and music. Assessment indicated that Brenda had non-verbal abilities within the average range but verbal abilities at the second centile.

Brenda was able to discuss her thoughts and feelings:
- She found it hard to respond to verbal teasing – a main reason for her change of secondary school.
- She avoided talking to adults because she did not always understand what they wanted of her.
- 'Teachers use big words when they explain things and set work' – she did not understand.
- Brenda stopped asking teachers to explain because she didn't understand the explanations: 'They get cross if you keep asking.'
- Others (students) can use big words to summarize when taking notes.
- Brenda's friends and her mother simplified their language so that she could understand. Her mother was not consciously aware before the assessment that she had been doing this for many years. 'Not got the words for it – happens all the time.'

Following the assessment Brenda's subject teachers were more aware of her needs and used strategies to support her learning. After school Brenda went to art college where she was successful.

It is often useful to ask subject teachers about how a student behaves in particular lessons. A behavioural questionnaire such as the one presented in Chapter 9 can reveal significant information about how a student responds in different subjects and to different teaching styles. Typical comments about a student who experiences comprehension problems might include:

- 'He disturbs others while I am talking.'
- 'He never knows what to do because he never listens.'

- 'He deliberately does the wrong thing – he can do it when I **show** him.'
- 'Noisy and disruptive in class, just a naughty boy.'
- 'He can read alright but he just doesn't seem to understand what he reads.'

'He' has been used in these statements because they were all made about boys. The gender ratio for SLCN is four boys to one girl, as for other neuro-developmental disorders.

The teacher's comments quoted focused on the surface behaviour that they had observed in the classroom. The last comment gives a more textured perspective and opens up the question about why he does not understand the text although he is able to read the words (decode). Some teachers are able to use the prompts offered by the behavioural questionnaire to make perceptive comments about students which are very helpful when attempting to analyze complex needs such as those of Brian.

Case study: Brian, Year 7

Teachers' responses to the behaviour questionnaire indicated that Brian was well behaved and appeared to be well motivated. He was able to speak with confidence in front of the class if he was given time and support to prepare the script. He enjoyed positive relationships with his peers, but often chose to work alone in class. One teacher described him as creative as he enjoyed art and music activities, but mostly out of school. Other staff commented on his:
- poor concentration, often in a 'world of his own', 'daydreams'
- limited ability to follow instruction
- low level of involvement in class discussions, seldom volunteering in response to questions
- problems starting tasks without support from LSA
- low confidence as learner.

One teacher had thought carefully about his problems and offered helpful insight which was used to inform the assessment procedures selected by the educational psychologist:
- 'He seems to struggle to understand.'
- 'His comprehension of what he has read is poor.'
- 'He needs instructions repeated to him several times in a simplified form.'
- 'He gets very agitated and frustrated with himself.'
- 'He needs constant one-on-one reassurance and prompting to stay focused on task.'

His mother provided supplementary information about Brian's high levels of anxiety, his reluctance to attend school and how she also had to simplify what she said to him.

When Brian was assessed using a standard battery of verbal and non-verbal tests, his non-verbal skills were found to be within the average range but he had difficulties with the processing/on-line analysis of complex incoming verbal information. Clinical analysis of his responses to verbal tasks indicated he also had problems with output:

- He needed extra time to organize his expressive language.
- Word-finding difficulties.
- Had difficulties with time concepts and sequencing which affected organization and time keeping within the school environment.

## Model of functioning for Brian: interventions

| Problem INPUT | | Problem OUTPUT |
|---|---|---|
| Listening with understanding difficulties | Internal representations Memory: Age appropriate (except for time concepts) | Expressing the main ideas of what he wants to say in sequence |
| Strategies Simplification of adult language Repetition | | Strategies Extra time to respond Pre-preparation of responses |
| Visual support | | Strategies to support word-finding difficulties |
| Support to get the main ideas in sequence | | Support to establish time concepts Getting the main ideas in sequence – narrative support/salience support |

Some students will welcome the opportunity to explain their own experiences in the classroom. Some may be defensive or not really know that they are not understanding at the same level as their classmates. For others, the habit of not listening or messing about in class has become entrenched and the notoriety of being sent out of lessons for fighting or being verbally abusive to teachers (Andy) can bring its own compensatory social rewards. The links between SLCN and behaviour are discussed in detail in Chapter 8.

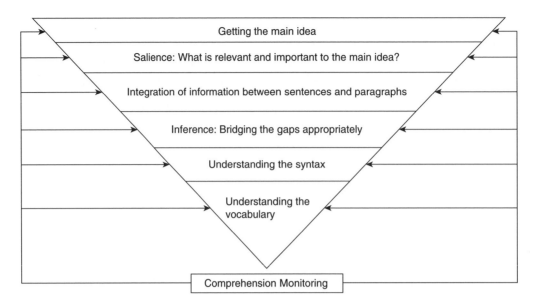

**Figure 2.1**   To understand a discourse or text.

Students who are aware of their difficulties may say:

- 'I don't understand what the teachers say, they use long words.'
- 'There's no point in reading it (text book), I don't understand so I don't do it.'
- 'I ask the others, not the teachers, then get into trouble for talking.'
- 'Teachers get fed up when I keep asking them.'
- 'I want to do it but I keep getting it wrong.'

A range of skills is involved in understanding what is said or what is written. These skills are represented schematically in Figure 2.1, which shows how the higher order skills are built on the more basic foundations. Each of the basic skills is discussed in turn, strategies to support learning in the classroom and specific strategies to support the development of all of the component skills are presented.

## 2.1 The basic skills

### 2.1.1 Listening

Listening may be more technically described as the ability to focus auditory attention and to sustain that attention over time. Most of us will automatically tune in to listen if we overhear our name or some key words relating to a topic we find particularly interesting. We are then able to select whether or not to focus our listening on what we have overheard. People vary in the degree to which they are then able to filter out distracting or competing stimuli, such as background noise, in order to sustain their listening. Students with ASC may find this phase of the process particularly difficult and students with ADHD may find it hard to sustain listening without being distracted. The more we need to make a conscious effort to listen, the harder it will be to sustain listening over time; for example, to a speaker who goes too quickly for us to process the information.

For students with SLCN their threshold for sustained listening may be particularly low because they do not expect to be able to understand and they have developed a habit of 'tuning out'. However, these same students who may show a very short listening attention span may be able to show a different level of ability to focus on non-verbal activities, tasks and topics that they find particularly interesting.

By the time students reach secondary school, unlearning the habits of not listening and developing better listening skills is inexorably linked to developing their understanding of what is said. Support strategies need to be put in place so that they begin to expect to be able to understand.

There are many games and activities that can be used to encourage good listening strategies. These are often used as whole class activities at primary school but are probably best introduced as part of a small group intervention programme at secondary school. Some of these activities are included with other ideas in Chapter 7 which discusses how to set up and manage social skills groups at secondary school.

## 2.1.2 Understanding vocabulary

In the introductory chapter, the section on language development discussed how some students may enter secondary school with quite limited vocabulary and word knowledge. Some words may have been learned and used in context; for example, the words 'Ancient Greece' might be familiar but they may not know that 'ancient' means 'old'. They may have weak semantic boundaries so that they may be aware that a 'stamp' is connected with letters, addresses, the mail and so on, but not know that the stamp pays for the postage. Students who have a limited understanding of common use vocabulary may find it particularly hard to learn:

- new vocabulary for naming objects (e.g. Bunsen burner)
- new concept words (e.g. digestive system)
- to attach a more specific meaning to words that they already know, such as:
  o force – make someone do something
  o force – as a term used in science.
- to develop a flexible understanding of words according to their context:
  o put it flat
  o he lives in a flat
  o flat bread.

Students with SLCN often have specific difficulties with certain concepts, particularly space or time concepts. The latter affected Brian and made it hard for him to operate the 2-week timetable that is used in his secondary school in order to be at the right place at the right time with the equipment he needed.

Other concepts may be difficult to understand, such as:

- contrasts (e.g. teach/learn, lend/borrow)
- language which changes according to the perspective of the person can be highly confusing
  - tomorrow, today will be yesterday/ today is yesterday's tomorrow.

It is important not to assume that students with SLCN understand the vocabulary that the rest of the group have mastered in primary school and to be aware that new subject-based vocabulary may have to be taught – it will not easily be picked up.

### 2.1.3 Understanding grammar

Some sentences are long and complex:

> 'If you have finished the diagram, you can begin to put away your apparatus but before starting the next exercise on page 7, copy the homework from the board so you get it down before the end of the lesson.'

Some sentences may be short but complex:

> 'The page the figures are on is at the end of the chapter.'

Even if students understand the basic vocabulary, they may struggle to process complex grammatical structures and if instructions are both long and complex, they may only carry out part of the instructions. Some specific grammatical forms may continue to cause additional problems for children with SLCN at secondary school:

- Negation: do not leave your worksheets on the table as you go out, you will need them for the homework
- Passives: the boy who was pushed in the queue needs to come to the Head of Year office
- Connectors: The difference in meaning can change according to the connector:
  - It was raining and **then** she went out (it stopped raining?)
  - It was raining **so** she went out (she likes the rain?).

Connectors are a source of implied meaning, which is one of the higher-level functions which is introduced in Figure 2.1.

## 2.2 Classroom approaches to support understanding

### 2.2.1 Classroom management

The social interactionist model of language (Barthorpe and Visser, 1991) highlights the importance of the match between the level of language that the teacher uses and the level of understanding of the student. Some strategies are easily incorporated into good classroom practice:

- Mark clearly when attentive listening is required. Some students may need an additional non-verbal prompt; for example, visual cue or hand on the desk to 'tune in'.
- Keep verbal instructions short and simple.
- Inter-weave directions and actions so that long sequences of language do not have to be processed without a break.
- Keep the **order of instruction** the same as the **order of action**.
- Identify the topic clearly, minimize topic change and signal any changes of topic; for example, when talking about an amoeba: 'That's what they look like, now we will talk about how they eat.'
- Repeat key sentences and ask the students to repeat back what they know/have to do.
- Clear consistent routines within the class will help students with comprehension or listening problems to anticipate expectations so there is less demand on listening skills. Introduce changes of the routine explicitly and support changes visually whenever possible. These strategies help to keep anxiety and arousal levels low and will support positive behaviour in the classroom.
- Use different levels of language combined with visual support in order to address the needs of a range of students. Most children with SLCN learn best when there is visual support for their learning. It is important to demonstrate, show and engage the students in experiential learning as much as possible.
- Research with students who have ADHD suggests that the use of signing and natural gesture may help students to sustain attention to the speaker (Wang *et al.*, 2004).

The Rupert technique (Ripley, 2006) combines the use of different levels of language with visual support (Figure 2.2). The Rupert technique is based on memories of the Christmas Annuals about Rupert the Bear. Each page had a picture, a rhyming couplet and some more dense text. The same principles can be applied to the presentation of information in class with the help of the interactive whiteboard or OHP.

### 2.2.2 Vocabulary in the classroom

Teachers always find the prospect of tape recording their lessons quite daunting, but when they are asked to do this as part of a training course,

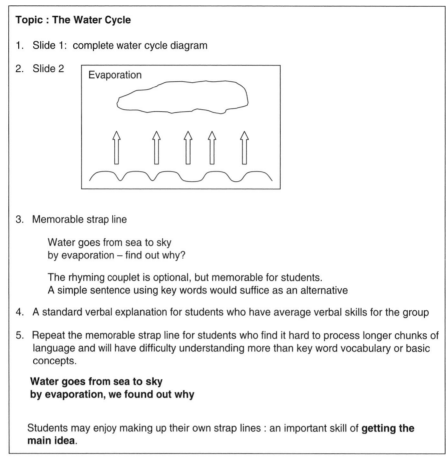

**Topic : The Water Cycle**

1. Slide 1: complete water cycle diagram

2. Slide 2

   Evaporation

3. Memorable strap line

   Water goes from sea to sky
   by evaporation – find out why?

   The rhyming couplet is optional, but memorable for students.
   A simple sentence using key words would suffice as an alternative

4. A standard verbal explanation for students who have average verbal skills for the group

5. Repeat the memorable strap line for students who find it hard to process longer chunks of language and will have difficulty understanding more than key word vocabulary or basic concepts.

   **Water goes from sea to sky
   by evaporation, we found out why**

   Students may enjoy making up their own strap lines : an important skill of **getting the main idea**.

**Figure 2.2**   An example of the Rupert technique.

they invariably say that it was a very useful exercise to do to pick up on key issues such as:

● Sentence length and complexity – simplification and re-wording can help some students such as Alice, Brenda and Brian.
● The vocabulary that is used: both content and process vocabulary. It is particularly important to be aware of social, common use vocabulary that is being used in a technical way or a more abstract way (see 'Understanding Vocabulary', p. 15).

Other words can be used in many different ways as a child gets older, according to the context. For example, the word 'light':

Early social use:          light vs. dark (an early contrast)

Use as a verb:            to light a match

More abstract, precise:   light vs. heavy (a later contrast)

Technical meanings:       white light (in science)

Figurative meaning:       light-fingered

The use of figurative language, such as metaphor, simile, analogy, parable and idioms can all be quite confusing for students who have limited vocabulary and understanding. They may take things surprisingly literally. Kerbel and Grunwell (2002) and Marshman (1998) have written more about teachers' use of figurative language and examples of commonly used figurative language are shown in Tables 2.1 and 2.2.

For every subject area some topic-specific vocabulary may have to be worked on in advance if students are going to be able to access the lesson. This is discussed in the section 'Specific Strategies for Students'.

There is always a dilemma for teachers when there is a need to keep core vocabulary constant for some students while extending and expanding the vocabulary of others. Teachers can accommodate both sets of needs and use alternative words for the same idea or concepts if they use word webs to support the students with difficulties.

Students with SLCN can focus on the core word, in the example the word 'field', and be assured that grazing and meadow are not two entirely different concepts.

**Table 2.1**   Idioms used 10 times or more in mainstream classes in primary school

All right
Take away
Get on
As well
Wait a minute
Hang on
Come on
Well done
Look for
In a minute
Write down
Make sure
Oh dear
Carry on
Now then
Put away
End up
Take your time
Sit down
Find out
Waste time
Write out

**Table 2.2** Figurative language

| Form | Example |
| --- | --- |
| Simile | He was as tall as a house |
| Metaphor | I lost the thread of the argument |
| Irony | That's great! |
| Idiom | Pull your socks up |
| Indirect request | Would you like to start your maths now? |

The use of word webs (Figure 2.3) in the teaching of vocabulary is discussed in the section about strategies for individual students.

### 2.2.3 Principles for curriculum delivery

In the section about language development in Chapter 1 (p. 6) the idea was introduced that children first learn a social language code and gradually develop the understanding and ability to use more complex, abstract, decontextualized language.

It is this language that is the main medium of instruction in the classroom and the language demands become greater as children move from key stage 1 through the other key stages. Lessons might be planned to intersperse tasks with higher cognitive demands with those which are less challenging.

## 2.3 Visual support for understanding in the secondary classroom

Students who experience difficulties with understanding the language that is used in the classroom because of limited word knowledge, limited

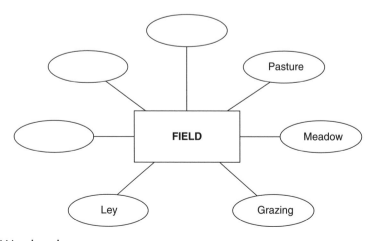

**Figure 2.3** Word web.

grammatical knowledge and/or slow processing of spoken language, will benefit from visual support for their learning.

Language comprehension at a word level and at a sentence level is supported by the triggering of relevant visual images. The process taps into a network of meaning that exists in our memories and links what we hear to what we already know and understand. Images are a more direct route for instant understanding than words. This is why road signs are in icon form – we can invest simple line drawings with a wealth of meaning.

Types of visual support in the secondary context may include:

- visual timetable which is an individualized version of the ubiquitous planner (Figure 2.4)
- a lesson schedule, whole class, group or individuals (Figure 2.5)
- a work schedule, whole class, group or individual (Figure 2.6)
- icons can be used for key words which represent universal concepts or topic-specific vocabulary
- Visual dictionaries for topics such as category dictionaries
- Worksheets using icons
- Topic and concept webs
- Diagrams to represent text
- Charts and graphs
- Revision guides using mind mapping

A sample lesson plan can be found on the website for Tourism and Leisure.

## 2.4 Strategies to support individual students

Even when strategies are in place to support learning in the classroom, some students will require additional individual support. This will often be

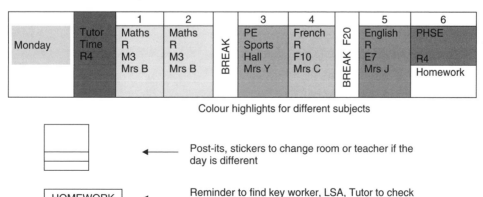

**Figure 2.4** An individual daily timetable.

## 2.   A Lesson Schedule

**On the student's desk/table**
**On the whiteboard**

| SUBJECT | TEACHER: |
|---|---|
|  | SUPPORT (LSA): |

1.    **Feedback from homework** (put in icon of house)

2.    **New Topic:  Norongoro Crater – Listen to Teacher** (put in icon of ear)

3.    **Watch video**  (put in icon of two eyes)

4.    **Discuss Video** (icon of two faces talking)

5.    **Learn Key Words**

6.    **Worksheet – write a sentence about the pictures** (picture of page of writing)

7.    **Homework:  Finish the sentences**

| SUBJECT | TEACHER: |
|---|---|
|  | SUPPORT (LSA): |

1.

2.

3.

4.

5.

6.

7.

**Figure 2.5**   A lesson schedule.

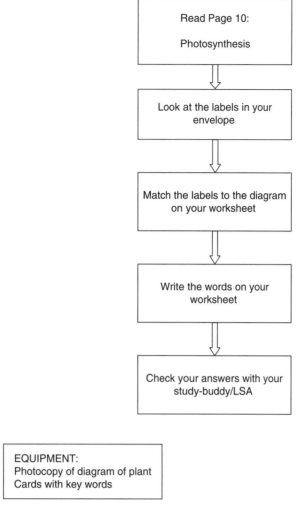

**Figure 2.6**   A work schedule.

delivered by support assistants as part of the individual education plan for the student(s). This section focuses on strategies that are tried and tested for use with individuals and small groups of students.

### 2.4.1 Learning vocabulary

One of the cornerstones of understanding is knowing the meaning of the key words that are used to guide the process of learning such as 'compare and contrast' as well as the content words that are relevant to the topic.

The first step is to identify the key words and concepts that the student needs to know. This mapping exercise (Figure 2.7) will be done by the LSA and subject teacher working in collaboration to identify key words and processes.

| SUBJECT: | DATE: |
|---|---|
| TEACHER: | TOPIC: |

**Key Words:**

**Process Words:**

*Classify*
*Summarize*
*Discuss*

**Extension Vocabulary**

**Figure 2.7** Mapping exercise to identify key words and concepts.

## 2.4.2 Strategies to teach new vocabulary

New vocabulary is best taught using a hierarchical approach (Rinaldi, 2005) so that the core vocabulary chosen will include topic/subject and category labels and be taught in a systematic way using the curriculum. The sequence suggested is as follows:

- Ensure the vocabulary and concept teaching is topic based. Teach related words grouped into sets, categories and items.
- Teach category labels; for example, vulcanicity, extrusive forms, volcanoes and the specific vocabulary and concepts within these.
- Always begin with the big picture; for example, land forms, volcanoes. Regularly refer back to this at the start of each lesson.
- Brainstorm the topic in a hierarchical way.
- Link learning to known events; for example, Pompeii, active volcanoes such as Mount Etna.
- Use vocabulary/concepts that are already known to the student in order to learn new vocabulary.
- Place in a context – link the vocabulary to real life situations whenever possible, and use real objects; for example, rock samples, go to real places, show video or pictures.
- Use multi-sensory reinforcement.
- Students describe words by meaning; for example, putting the item into its group category and by attributes such as shape, size, colour and so on.
- Make sure words are learned correctly with reference to their sound structure.
- The most complex and subtle vocabulary; for example, exceptions. Ambiguity should not be introduced until the key groups have been learned.
- Provide opportunities for a lot of reinforcement and repetition of key words; that is, revisit the vocabulary even when the topic is finished and reinforce the vocabulary concepts in as many different contexts as possible.

## 2.5  Working with text

Many students who have SLCN in secondary school and have not been reclassified as dyslexic will have decoding skills that are in advance of their understanding of either spoken or written language. These hyperlexic students who have semantic problems but relatively strong phonological systems and adequate social and pragmatic skills may, like Andy and Alice, have their difficulties masked through primary school. Students who do have adequate decoding skills can benefit from strategies that use text to develop their basic and higher level comprehension skills. Written language, unlike spoken language, does not disappear before it is fully processed.

Students who are able to read are exposed to a greater range of complex vocabulary that is not often used in conversation. Any written material can, therefore, be used to audit and teach new vocabulary. Also, it is by reading that students are exposed to more complex, formal grammar than is used in spoken language. Analyzing the written language of a student can give important clues about their understanding and use of syntax. It may be necessary to teach some students syntactical features such as the rules for joining sentences. We will discuss how to teach these in the section about expressive language. However, it is only when the students use these forms appropriately and flexibly that we can be certain that they understand them.

Students who have difficulty with comprehension can be helped to access text by pre-preparation of the text. This might be done in the classroom with a small group or with an individual.

**Pre-preparation of text** would include a range of activities:

- introduction of new vocabulary using the techniques already described to link the new words to a network of meaning
- identification of any common use vocabulary that has more precise, specific meaning in the context of the text
- discussion about the use of connectors and how they affect the meaning of the text; try out some alternative connectors
- explain and simplify any complex sentences and grammatical structures; for example the passive form
- clarify the sequence of events in the text – draw them in order using icons to clarify the sequence and make it more memorable
- clarify the main ideas; strategies to do this are presented in the relevant section
- identify and explain inferences
- practice prediction.

The pre-preparation of the text will in many cases involve the simplification of the text. The use of a diagram to clarify the text will help some students. For some texts it may help to re-order the content so that the events are put in a simple time sequence or that the order of mention in an instruction matches the order of action. These sequences can be represented in flow diagrams to make them more accessible.

A particular area of difficulty for some students may be the language that is used in examinations or test questions. It is helpful to work with students to break down the questions into a more accessible form.

Q: 'There were many consequences of Hitler's invasion of Poland. Outline the causes of this course of action and their effect.'

Analysis:

- Why did Hitler invade Poland? List the causes.
- Describe what happened after Hitler invaded Poland.
- What did the invasion make other countries do?

It may be helpful to work with all students to clarify and simplify what is required in response to common forms of wording that is used in exam questions. Once they have practiced with adult guidance they can try the exercise for themselves. This type of preparation has a good 'pay-off' in terms of exam grades.

## 2.6  Getting the main ideas and sequencing the ideas

Working with text provides a good opportunity to help students with salience. Many students with SLCN may be diverted from the main argument or threads of the narrative by details that are not particularly important. Often these details have a resonance with something that they understand, have experienced or trigger a particular area of interest.

### 2.6.1  Key wording

Strategies such as key wording may help students to focus on the main ideas. An example of key wording from a neurological text is given on the website.

Some students may prefer to use highlighter pens to key word text. This can be particularly useful when key wording a text with dialogue or a play script. Different characters can be given their own colour code. Similarly, when picking out arguments for or against a plan or idea as represented in a text, use one colour for arguments in favour, and another colour for arguments against. The main points are then collated in a table (e.g. Figure 2.8).

| For  (green) | Against (red) |
|---|---|
| •    List main ideas<br><br>•<br><br>• | •    List main ideas<br><br>•<br><br>• |

**Figure 2.8**  Main ideas.

## 2.6.2 Choose a title

Another strategy for distilling the main ideas from a text is to use titles for paragraphs or sections. Students may start to learn this technique by selecting a title which best represents a story sequence from a multiple choice. Any picture sequence can be used to practice the technique.

Once students are fluent with the technique they can generate their own titles which summarize the main ideas of a picture sequence. The third phase of the training is to support the students to get the main idea of a paragraph and make a title to summarize the information. A summary for the neurological text on the website might be:

Summary of text

The hands and mouth, which make the most precise movements, are controlled by the largest area of the motor cortex.

*The Human Brain – a Guided Tour, Susan Greenfield*


## 2.6.3 Making inferences

People with good language skills make inferences all the time without being aware that this is what they are doing. They pick up on implied meanings and indirect requests because of their understanding of the social world and how other people think and behave. For example, if our partner says 'It's getting late' – it may mean s/he wants to go home.

We infer meanings from our knowledge of other people and from the context. Similarly, in text not all the details are given and we must pick up on the cues we have available in order to fully understand the meaning. Students with SLCN, especially those who have social communication difficulties, may have particular problems with inference.

It is possible to start teaching inference in a structured way. Even a single sentence can be analyzed by discussing what individual words can tell us about the meaning and the implied meaning.

Once the students have worked on sentences you might use simple verbal or written paragraphs that are structured in order to make the inferences more obvious. Some students may need the text or story to be illustrated with icons as the story is told or read to them. An example of a simple text to discuss inference can be found on the website.

After practicing using structured texts, it is possible to graduate to working together on selected published texts and to use standard comprehension exercises that involve inference.

### 2.6.4 Comprehension monitoring

Students with speech and language impairment (SLI) who are able to decode text quite efficiently may, nevertheless, fail to notice and self-correct decoding errors which are not consistent with the meaning or context of the sentence or paragraph; for example,

He put the    (chair) on his bike to fasten it to the    (road)

         chain                                            rail

These students need support to focus on the meaning of the text and, usually, what is said to them. By key stage 3, students may not expect to make sense out of what they hear or read and just hope to 'get by' with understanding the key words that they do recognize.

A technique can be used to help students to monitor for meaning what is said. It follows a simple format and the sentences and paragraphs can be spoken by the adult and/or read by the student. The aim is for students to identify inconsistencies in the script and examples of comprehension monitoring exercises can be found on the website.

Adults who work with the students can use and adapt any text that they are using in a lesson to provide comprehension monitoring practice. It is often helpful to photocopy the text, highlight the words you want to change and write in the word that you intend to substitute for the original word. If you try to improvise there will be pauses in the reading which will give the students cues that you are changing a word. If you are working with a written text, the students can have a copy of the altered text and use a highlighter to mark the inconsistencies. The exercise can then be discussed with the individual or with a group of students.

> **Points to remember**
>
> - Students with a history of SCLN may not expect to understand and often develop avoidance strategies for when focused listening is expected.
> - Talking to teachers and students about things that the student is successful at and things that they find difficult can provide clues about their level of understanding.

- Students may have difficulties understanding vocabulary, grammar or both.
- There are ways that the learning environment of the classroom can be adapted to support students who have comprehension difficulties and visual support is often very effective.
- Some students may benefit from a more individual intervention programme and, if they can decode text, written language may be used to support understanding.

# 3

# Remembering Memory

> **Chapter Objectives**
>
> > To understand memory as a three-phase process
> > To explain the different forms of memory and how individuals' memory profiles have strengths and weaknesses
> > To show how students with SLCN often have relatively weak auditory memory systems and how other aspects of their memory systems may be harnessed to support learning
> > To provide strategies to support the three phases of memory in the classroom
> > To discuss strategies for students who have specific problems with the recall of information including how to recognize word-finding difficulties

## 3.1 The memory process

Memory is defined as the ability to take in, store and retrieve information. It can take many different forms, most of which we take for granted unless there is a breakdown in our memory system because of some trauma such as a stroke or the development of Alzheimer's disease. Under these circumstances the awareness of forgetting can be very frustrating for the individual. However, we can only forget information that has been acquired as a memory and has been stored in our brains. Every day our senses register a mass of information to which we choose not to attend and acquire as a memory. Thus, we may focus our attention on one man in the railway carriage who is noisily chatting on a mobile telephone and be able to recognize him later, but not have any recognition or recall memory for the rest of the people we sat near. This example illustrates how we all continuously filter out a lot of information that is not judged as important and make active decisions about what we will attend to and remember, or try to remember. Without this ability to prioritize the information received by our senses and filter out information we do not register as important, we would be swamped by the volume of incoming sensory information that needed to be processed. There are theories that suggest that some children on the autistic spectrum have difficulties filtering out and prioritizing incoming sensory information.

The evidence suggests that memory is a three-stage process:

- the acquisition phase, which involves an active focus on what is to be remembered
- the retention phase, which involves processing the information and coding it for storing
- the retrieval phase, which may take the form of recognition or the more demanding recall process.

In this chapter we will discuss teaching strategies that will help a student at each stage of the process and strategies that students may use to help themselves to remember information.

First, however, it is important to consider the many different forms that memory may take. Most people will recognize that their own memory system is stronger in some areas than in others. One goal for adults working with children will be to help them to discover the areas of relative strength in their own memory system and how they may use these strengths to support their learning. Casey was despaired of by her teachers at primary school because she found it hard to retain the core skills needed for making progress with reading and number work. By working with Casey and talking about some of the activities she enjoyed and her experiences of success, it was possible to identify the strengths in her memory system and use these to support her learning.

## 3.2 Types of memory

There are many different types of memory which are encoded in different parts of the brain. We now know that memories for facts and experiences are usually encoded verbally (semantic memory) and stored in the part of the brain known as the hippocampus. They are maintained there for as long as 2–3 years with the aid of rehearsal (recalling the information), before passing it to the temporal lobe of the cortex for long-term storage.

Memory can take many forms and the first section explores the memories which focus on the integration of personal experience. For different people, and for different situations, visual, auditory, kinaesthetic and even the taste and smell senses may dominate these memories.

### 3.2.1 Autobiographical and episodic memory

Most people have a store of autobiographical personal memories which contribute to the narrative they construct about their lives. In cases of amnesia – known as fugue – the loss of these memories that add up to our sense of personal identity can be distressing and disorientating.

When an audience is asked to recall memories of their first day at school or first date, most people are able to recount some aspect of these experiences. Some people recall tastes, sounds, sights or feelings with various levels of intensity. However, cross-referencing with siblings, parents or classmates can give us clues about how our memories – our perspective on the events – are idiosyncratic and may have evolved over time. The work of Bartlett (1932) demonstrated how people recall changes over time and how the memories of events are altered to fit in with cultural and social expectations. We may also manicure our memories of events to fit with our current personal narratives without being aware that we are doing so.

There are some national or international events that impose common episodic memories such as where you were when you heard that the aeroplanes had hit the Twin Towers, or Princess Diana had died in a car crash.

We all recall events that we, or others who we know, have experienced and in this way episodic memory often overlaps with our autobiographical memories. One of the earliest mnemonic techniques relied on personal memories of place by linking new information to be learned to objects positioned around a familiar room. In a modern context we can still use these personal memory strengths to support learning.

### 3.2.2 Procedural memories

Some people are much better than others at remembering how to do things. If you don't often need to put oil in your car, or usually get someone else to do it, you may forget from one event to another how to open the car bonnet. If you do the procedures frequently it is hard to understand how other people can forget them. Regular practice is usually the answer – doing it yourself first with a coach at hand and then independently. The example about cars is not immediately relevant in the classroom but procedural memory is implicated in how we remember to do procedures at school; for example, how to do long division.

The evidence from the neurologists suggests that procedural memories, the 'how to' memories, involve a different area of the brain from the 'what?' factual memories. The neural loop for 'how to' involves the cerebellum and the subcortical nucleus known as the putamen. This 'how to' mechanism appears to be less susceptible to degeneration than memories encoded by the hippocampus and may persist when other memories are severely disrupted, as in Alzheimer's disease.

If there is a problem with procedural memory, visual support in the form of a flow diagram may provide the necessary back up. Casey had significant difficulties with procedural memory and two strategies were helpful to her:

- a rhythmic chant for the steps in the procedure
- visual support using flow charts.

 Examples of flow charts are included in 'Strategies' (Chapter 2).

### 3.2.3 Motor memories

One of the most fundamental forms of memory is how we all learn and remember how to move our bodies in space in order to perform voluntary movements. As adults we are mostly not consciously aware of the learning and practice that was involved in learning how to carry out commonplace activities such as walking but we may be reminded when something goes wrong; for example, with a broken arm, the motor movement patterns that we have learned are no longer functional.

Adults have learned motor plans which ensure that their movements are efficient with smooth transitions and sequenced between the movements.

One of the complex motor plans that is in place for the majority of adults is the ability to handwrite fluently and efficiently. The learned motor plan enables people to write familiar words without having to attend to the details of individual letter formation or spacing.

Try the effectiveness of your motor plan by shutting your eyes and writing your name and address. Then swap hands and try the same thing with your non-preferred hand that does not have the motor plan and see the difference.

Children with dyspraxia may, of course, find it hard to establish the effective, efficient motor plans for writing (Ripley *et al.*, 1997). However, for students who are able to develop effective, efficient motor plans, these can also be used to support other learning; for example, the cover–copy–write technique for teaching spelling follows this strategy. Memories for most skilled motor movements are stored in the cerebellum but those that involve intricate hand movements are stored and co-ordinated in the motor cortex. Motor memories seem to be particularly enduring – we don't forget how to ride a bike or rise to trot on a horse once we have acquired the motor plans.

### 3.2.4  Splinter memory systems

Three particular types of memory appear to have developed in a rather different way, perhaps because of their evolutionary significance:

- navigational memory which is useful for a hunter gatherer
- face recognition and, separately, the recognition of facial expressions both of which are useful for an animal living in a social group
- the memory for emotionally charged events which are linked to the primitive flight or fight response are stored in the amygdala. Memory for facts (involving the hippocampus): 'That is a bull not a cow.' Memory for affect (involving the amygdala): 'I am scared of bulls – run!'

### 3.2.5  The visual and auditory systems

The visual memory system is important for personal, episodic memory, for early or emotionally charged events and for face recognition. Visual images may give support to procedural and navigational memory. However, once an individual has developed language, most memories are recoded verbally and stored as part of the semantic and phonological memory systems. It is clear from this that people who have difficulties with language are likely to rely on visual memory systems to a greater extent than others.

What is known about memory systems suggests that the visual and auditory systems are closely linked. Both the visual and auditory memory systems consist of several different components. Our knowledge of the details of the different visual systems is still emerging. The auditory system consists of different components which include:

- the phonological system, which coordinates the storing and recall of the sounds in words (discussed in Chapter 5)
- voice recognition, analogous to face recognition in the visual system, which supports the identification of people and 'reading' their mood
- sound recognition for non-verbal information – musicians, mechanics and physicians have their own 'dictionary' of salient sounds.

Most information from the auditory system is subsequently encoded verbally and stored in the semantic memory, which involves the hippocampus.

The discussion about the different types of memory has emphasized the complexity of the concept known generically as 'memory' and how different parts of the memory system are associated with different parts of the brain. The corollary of this is that it is possible to use strengths in one area to compensate for relative weaknesses in other areas. For students with SLCN their relative weakness is likely to be in the auditory memory system, which is the most efficient and effective system for people who do not have SLCN. For Casey, her relatively strong visual and semantic systems were used to support her weaker procedural and phonological systems.

## 3.3 Support for memory: strategies for the classroom

Students who find it hard to remember what we tell them and appear to fail to learn in the context of the curriculum, can be quite frustrating for any teacher. The comments that teachers make sometimes reflect that frustration:

- 'I think he has really got it one day, but next lesson he's back to square one.'
- 'When I ask him to tell me the task, he just repeats back the last bit of what I said.'
- 'He never remembers his books or his homework.'

The classroom strategies that teachers might use are presented under the three headings of the stages of the system: acquisition, storage and retrieval.

### 3.3.1 Acquisition

The strategies to support acquisition are essentially the same as those which are used to facilitate comprehension:

- the use of a range of presentation techniques which include the visual strategies that are presented in Chapter 2
- encouraging the students to notice as much as possible about the information (this type of technique is explained in detail in the section about word finding)
- deciding what is most salient (getting the main idea – Chapter 2)
- the way in which the item/event is similar or different from others that have been previously introduced
- use different experiential techniques such as active learning through role play, demonstration followed by supervised practice of the sequences of a task
- ensure that the student's attention is engaged at the onset and refocusing their attention by highlighting the most important information, as with the Rupert technique (p. 18)

- modification of the language of instruction (see Chapter 2)
- linking new learning to what the student(s) already knows, which can be done with the class, group or an individual
- work in pairs or small groups to pool knowledge or remember from a previous session and sharing this with the larger group
- modify the learning environment to minimize distractions from the material that is to be learned
- engage students in discussion about what they remember well and help them to understand their memory system. This will help to develop meta-cognition – what is the best way for me to learn this type of material. Some individual strategies are presented in the section 'Support for memory: strategies for learners' (p. 29)
- the more students actively engage with the material, the more likely they are to remember it. This is particularly true when you are working with text as we all make additions or changes to a text we need to remember to make it more memorable:
  o underlining
  o highlighting
  o notes in the margin
  o add sub-headings
  o recast the material as a diagram or mind map.

Students can be encouraged to use these strategies themselves.

### 3.3.2 Retention of information

In order to learn, the information that has been acquired must be stored and retained over time in a form that can be retrieved. Teachers may help students to remember what they have been taught by the following methods:

- Presenting the information that needs to be learned at the start and end of the session because memory tends to show both primacy and recency effects. Students may remember best what they heard first (primacy effect) or what they heard last (recency effect).
- Attention is most likely to wane in the middle of a session so this is the opportunity for more active, hands-on, practical strategies.
- Introduce listening breaks by presenting the material visually or through more experiential techniques, but revise and recall the key information after each listening break.
- Include opportunities for rehearsal and repetition in the structure of the lesson. Subsequently, it is helpful to review and revise modules that students have already learned, to use the information in different contexts for a purpose and link information to any relevant new learning.
- Students will remember information from a text more effectively if they have the opportunity to work on the text during, or soon after, reading it.

These activities might include note-taking, key wording, summarizing and finding appropriate titles for each paragraph.

- Students may be asked to respond individually or in small groups to key questions about a text in order to focus on the meaning.
  - Does the text relate to anything you know about already?
  - How does the text relate to this previous knowledge?
  - Does it support what you already think or know, or does it challenge it?
  - How may any differences be resolved?

As a group exercise this format works well and the ideas may be recorded in a mind map format.

### 3.3.3 Retrieval

There are two retrieval systems that operate for us all: **recognition** and **recall**. We are aware that when we meet a person and recognize them the context will affect the ease with which we are able to greet them by name. Research is able to demonstrate the difference between the systems involved in recognition and recall. Mandler *et al.* (1969) gave subjects 100 words to learn. When their memories for the words were tested after the same amount of rehearsal and practice time, the recall group were on average correct 38% of the time, but the recognition group 96% of the time.

The research on memory also gives us some clues about how cueing can be used to support the recall of information. Cueing techniques that have been found to be effective include:

- Visual imaging – the most powerful form of cueing. The person links what is to be learned to a visual image.
- Semantic cueing – for example, giving the category that the information relates to.
- Paired cueing – learning target words paired with another word, the cue is the non-target pair word.
- Contextual support – people remember things best when they recall them in the same context as when they learned the information. Some people use this strategy spontaneously as when they return to the place where they thought about what they needed from upstairs, but had forgotten when they got upstairs.
- Mood variables – Teasdale and Fogarty (1979) demonstrated that mood can affect recall. When people are sad they remember more sad events.
- Recall is aided when the new information is linked to what is already known so that the information becomes part of a whole network of meaning.

If there are more links to the target information it is possible to use a range of self-cueing techniques – there is not just one route to recall.

Teachers can make recall easier for students:

- Allow time for a student to use self-cueing strategies when they are trying to recall something specific.
- Avoid asking a student with accessing/recall difficulties questions that they have not had time to think about beforehand in front of the group.
- Provide cues for the student.
- Help them to think about the context in which the learning took place.
- Activate the links to what they already knew about the topic.
- Provide visual cues.
- Give forced alternatives which build on the principle that recognition is easier than recall and practice of recognition/recall builds the recall pathways for next time.
- Offer different modes for recall, not just verbal recall, to reduce the pressure on spoken language for students with SLCN, for example draw it, demonstrate it or mime it.
- In the group, elicit the first steps of a sequence of events such as remembering how to do an experiment, the first two of Henry VIII's wives, and so on, and ask the students with difficulties to contribute once the sequential context has been established.

## 3.4 Support for memory: strategies for learners

Semantic, verbal and/or phonological memory are usually the most problematic for students with SLCN. Unfortunately for them, these are the forms of memory which underpin much of the formal learning that goes on in the classroom. One of the most common, and frustrating, manifestations may be specific word-finding difficulties and this is also discussed in Chapter 6. The ways in which visual memory, kinaesthetic/motor memory, procedural memory and episodic/personal memory can be used to support verbal memory and how verbal memory itself can be supported are discussed in the sections that follow.

### 3.4.1 Word retrieval problems

We have all experienced word retrieval problems, often at crucial moments in our lives, when we have that 'tip of the tongue' feeling but can't come up with the word that we need. At a low level of incidence it can be irritating but when it happens frequently it can be highly frustrating and even affect the confidence with which we interact with other people, particularly if we suspect that we may be asked an unexpected question. This might happen routinely in a classroom with the additional stress of the presence of an audience of peers. It is not surprising, therefore, that some students with word-finding problems become reluctant communicators and avoid verbal encounters.

Other students with word retrieval problems may not inhibit their attempts to communicate, but when we listen to what they say their language may sound different or unusual. We may become aware of:

- A lot of pauses, hesitations and restarts in their speech, often with the use of 'fillers' such as 'um', 'you know' and so on.
- Some circumlocution, which is when a specific word can't be accessed and the student gives a description of the object or describes its function (e.g. target word 'buttercup' – 'it's got a long, green stem and is yellow in fields.' Surprisingly this child did recall a very specific word 'stem' quite successfully.) This strategy may give a rambling, unfocused impression of their language.
- If the student has problems with semantic recall, they may substitute a word from the same semantic field (e.g. 'watch' for 'clock'). In some cases this will not substantially affect the meaning of what they want to say, but other times the substituted word may not fit in the context of the rest of the sentence.
- If a student has problems with their phonological memory, they may well substitute words which sound the same as the target word (e.g. 'bottle' for 'battle').
- Students' language may be peppered with non-specific words such as 'it' (with no reference point), 'thingy' or 'whatsit'.
- Some words such as the verb 'do', or the noun 'stuff' may be used as a generic for a whole range of more specific verbs and nouns.
- Revisions and repetitions, for example 'We went to the zoo and saw, er, we saw (pause and sigh) them, we went on a train.'
- Non-verbal signs of frustration about not being able to word-find are very common; they can include the subtle signs – sighs, frowns, shrugs of the shoulder, but at the extreme even banging the head with the hand or on the desk.
- Some students may abandon their attempt to communicate – they start an explanation or description, are unable to access a key word(s) and resort to 'Dunno' or 'Can't remember.'

Some people find it hard to remember the phonological code for a word that they want to use. They know the meaning but are unable to remember how to say it. Visual cueing may help to support the memory of the phonological code as demonstrated in Figure 3.1.

For other people it is not the phonological code that is insecure but there is a tenuous link between the phonological code and the semantic memory that stores word knowledge. The person can remember the word but is unable to put a meaning to that word. Visual imaging can help with this problem too.

**Day 1**

- Read the word on an email.
- Look it up in the dictionary, partly to engage in active learning.

**Day 2**

- Know the meaning of the word (i.e. semantic memory is working well), but only able to recall part of the phonological code

Con  tion

- Tell a wordsmith the meaning and he supplies the word 'concatanation'
- Recall strategy

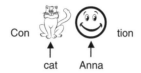

Con    tion

cat    Anna

**After Day 2**

- The word can now be cued by the icons as and when required

**Figure 3.1**   Example of visual cueing to support a phonological memory problem.

## 3.4.2  Visual support for memory

It is possible to identify students who have a strong visual memory that may be used to support their learning, as shown by Colin.

 Case study: Colin, Year 7

Colin had severe oral–verbal dyspraxia which made it hard for him to understand or use language. His teachers were concerned about his educational progress because the language impairment made it difficult for him to demonstrate what he had learned through the verbal medium. He had the sequencing difficulties associated with dyspraxia, so procedural memory was weak even for processes such as subtraction which he had been working on for years. His more general dyspraxia also ruled out motor memory as a way of supporting his learning.

The decision was made to investigate his visual memory. A task had to be found that did not have a significant motor output component because of his dyspraxia and visual memory tasks from the British Ability Scales (BAS) were selected for the assessment.

Colin performed at first centile for the recall under the conditions of both immediate and delayed verbal recall. However, Colin performed the visual recall making only one error and it was how he performed the task that was so impressive.

- He was confident and relaxed – unlike his response under the conditions of verbal recall.
- He took the cards in order from the top of the shuffled pack and placed them on the blank grid with a fluency and speed that was most impressive.

Colin was clearly a very strong visual learner and his quite exceptional skills in this area were subsequently used to good effect in his learning programmes when he transferred to secondary school.

### 3.4.2.1 Visual imaging

Visual support for memory is very important as demonstrated by Bristow (1999) when 96% of students in a Brighton secondary school reported using pictures in their head to support learning. One of the earliest visual strategies that is described in the literature is constructing a visual image of the information that is to be learned. Clearly, from Bristow's research, most people carry out some visual imaging spontaneously but the skill can be taught and practiced by students. Some of the well-known 'memory-men' use visual imaging as a key strategy.

### 3.4.2.2 An example of imaging

A student attempting to remember the sequence of plant forms on a mountain might imagine, and describe verbally, a walk from the flat valley floor through the grass to the wooded slope ('What trees can you see?'), to the heather moor ('What does it feel like on your bare legs?') to the barren rock outcrops with some green lichen and a few hardy plants clinging to the cracks. The student 're-walks' the path in their head with or without a verbalization in order to learn the facts. When the information needs to be recalled, the student re-walks the route and draws or describes what they see.

The construction of images is a very personal experience. We can help students to discover the process of imaging but the pictures inside their heads must be their own. The cued spelling programme (Topping, 2001) makes use of the power of visual imagery. Icon note taking, as described in Chapter 2, is also a way of linking picture cues to a text and the icons may be easier for the student to remember so that they can serve as visual cues for recalling the text at a later date.

### 3.4.2.3 Visual support for procedures

A procedure in this context is how you go about completing a task – like carrying out a standard process like testing the pH of the soil or how to complete a mathematical process such as working out a percentage.

All these types of activity can be broken down into smaller steps by the process known as 'task analysis'. The order in which these steps need to be tackled can then be set out in the form of a flow chart.

In the first instance the adult will take the lead to carry out the task analysis and record the steps on the flow chart. The student works through the stages with adult support as necessary. Once the student is familiar with the procedure of task analysis, individuals or groups of students can carry out the task analysis with the support of an adult. The aim is that the student will become independent, not only for completing the task or procedure, but also for carrying out the process of task analysis. The skill can then be generalized to any procedure that the student needs to carry out. Task analysis is often useful for mathematical processes or how to complete an independent task.

An example of two task analyses are presented as illustrations:

- A procedural flow chart of how to do percentages is shown in Figure 3.2.
- A work schedule to complete an independent task is shown in Figure 3.3.

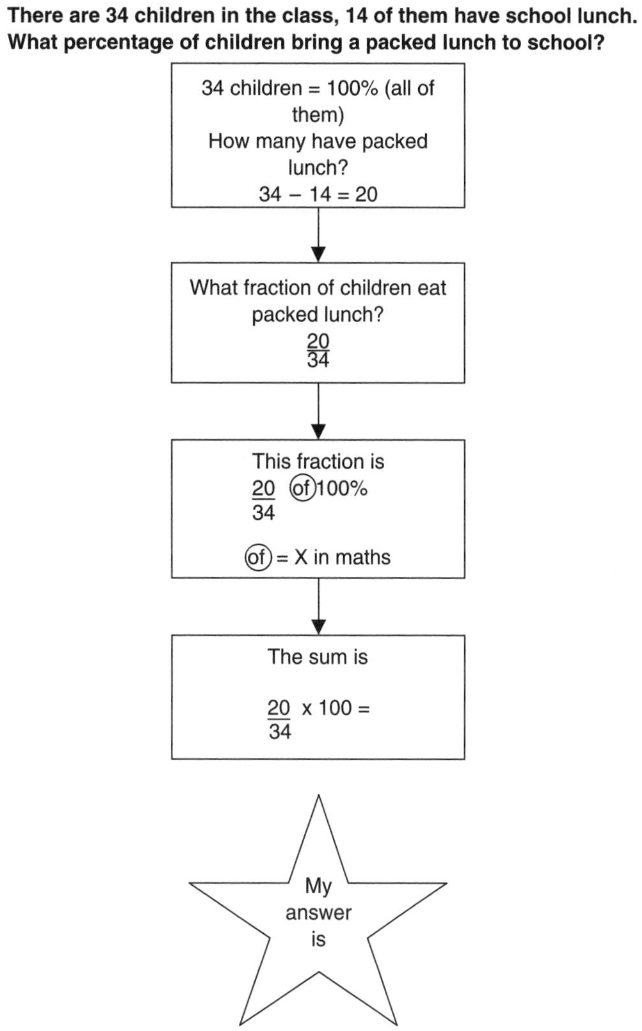

**There are 34 children in the class, 14 of them have school lunch.**
**What percentage of children bring a packed lunch to school?**

34 children = 100% (all of them)
How many have packed lunch?
34 − 14 = 20

What fraction of children eat packed lunch?
$\frac{20}{34}$

This fraction is
$\frac{20}{34}$ (of) 100%

(of) = X in maths

The sum is

$\frac{20}{34}$ x 100 =

My answer is

**Figure 3.2** A procedural flow chart for percentages.

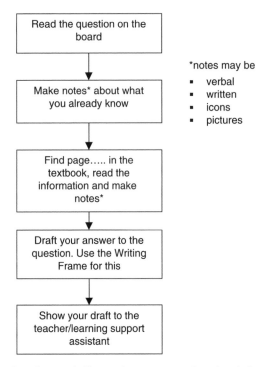

**Figure 3.3** An example of a task flow chart or work schedule.

Staff in secondary schools have found it useful to have copies of flow chart templates with a flexible number of stages. Laminated versions of the flow charts for procedures that students may often need – the 'how to do' sheets – can be prepared in advance and consulted when needed. Examples include 'How to do long division,' 'How to carry out a litmus test' and 'How to find a grid reference.'

We all routinely use visual schedules every day – our diaries and calendars – and would be lost without them. Students are expected to follow their timetables and planners to remember where they need to be and what subjects to have their books for. Some students will benefit from more explicit visual support for organization and many forms of visual timetables and work schedules are in regular use in secondary school. They are often first put in place to meet the needs of students on the autistic spectrum, but prove invaluable to support a range of students, including those who are not on the special needs register.

### 3.4.3 Non-visual strategies to support memory

Most of the chapter has been devoted to visual strategies because these are often the preferred option for students with SLCN. However, other forms of memory may be the choice of some students for some tasks.

- Kinaesthetic memory
  - Learning skills by practice and building the motor plan; for example, handwriting, typing, accessing websites, following science methods.
  - Doing with saying: as for simultaneous oral spelling.
  - Walking the memory: linking what needs to be learned to objects or places in a room and walking the room in the correct order to aid recall.
  - Attach a sign or action to an instruction or word. The cued articulation technique (Passey, 1985) used by speech and language therapists uses this technique for sounds.
- Episodic memory
  - Link new learning to familiar places – combined with imaging technique.
  - Field trips and visits to reinforce classroom learning.
  - Put new facts into a narrative form, even using a life path narrative.
  - Change where the students sit and link new learning to the change of place, position, neighbour. This can then be used for self-cueing; for example, 'What I learned working with …'.
- Verbal memory. Reinforce verbal memory itself by
  - Rehearsal.
  - Making up silly rhymes and sentences as with the Rupert technique.
  - Write lists.
  - Categorize and classify materials – as with word webs and hierarchies as discussed in Chapter 2.
  - Link new learning to what is already known – build up the network of learning.
  - Use verbal mnemonics – visual reinforcement optional; for example, GHOST (**G**hosts **H**ate **O**ranges **S**ausages **T**ea).

### 3.4.4 A reviewing system to support retention

A reviewing system has been developed by Mitchell (2003) for students who learn facts one day and have forgotten them by the next lesson. It can help students to learn spellings, timetables, vocabulary, concepts or definitions and help them become more independent in their learning.

Research has shown that adults forget as much as 80% of information learned within a day, unless the information is of particular personal interest. The idea of this system is that information is reviewed at regular intervals so that it eventually stays in the student's long-term memory. Readers who are interested might consult www.time2revise.co.uk – a computer programme for key stages 1–3 (key stage 4 is also available) by Jane Mitchell of the Communication and Language Skills Centre (CALSC).

## Points to remember

- The different types of memory and how areas of strength within a student's memory system can be used to support their learning.
- The important role of visual support for students who have SLCN. Visual imaging is a powerful tool but the helpful images will be unique for each student.
- Acquisition of memories can be improved by selecting the optimum way of presenting the information to the student by matching to their memory strengths.
- The importance of using/rehearsing memories to enhance long-term retention.
- A student does not have to use language to demonstrate what they know.

# Thinking Language

**Chapter Objectives**

> To demonstrate the key role of language skills in the process of thinking
> To explore different types of thinking
> To outline the difficulties that students with SLCN may experience with thinking
> To outline the different ways in which thinking skills may be taught
> To describe the strategies which are most useful for students with SLCN

Vygotsky (1962) described the stages in the development of 'private speech', which is the self-talk that is used to guide behaviour. Students who have SLCN do not easily develop this private speech, a function of language that is also the main vehicle for thinking. They will therefore have problems with thinking skills that involve:

- planning what they mean to do
- working towards long-term goals
- sequencing ideas – a narrative skill
- reflecting on what has happened or acquired knowledge
- speculating what might happen if …
- selecting information that is salient.

However, thinking is a process and, as such, may be learned.

The evidence from De Bono (2000) and others suggests that teaching the relevant skills can improve the thinking skills of all students.

## 4.1  Promoting thinking skills

We are constantly reminding children that they must 'think', without ever explaining what we are asking them to do and what we mean by 'thinking'.

We use the word 'think' all the time. It might be:

- 'I think it's time to go home' – making a decision.
- 'I think it's going to rain' – predicting.
- 'I think the train would be better than taking the bus or car' – analyzing.
- 'I think what he said to you was dreadful' – empathizing.
- 'I think there's a better way of thinking this through' – thinking about thinking.

To 'think' is an abstract concept that is manifested in many ways. The examples given are just a few.

De Bono says that to be effective, thinking does not require a huge information base as vast amounts of information do not do our thinking for us. He suggests that given an effective structure for thinking, everyone, even those with an inadequate information base, can potentially be a better thinker. This 'information base' though is dependent on language, which is our primary tool for most types of thinking, although not all thinking requires the medium of language; for example, music and art.

However, language is the tool for most types of thinking, particularly within the educational setting and this immediately places students with SLCN at a disadvantage. Not only do they struggle to acquire an adequate information base, but further meta-linguistic language skills associated with CALP (Chapter 1) need to be learned in order to become an effective thinker. Even the simplest language needed for thinking may need to be simplified. Use the word 'predict' and you will be greeted with a row of blank faces, but discuss 'what might happen', and this enables students with SLCN to begin to understand.

## 4.2  Why teach thinking skills?

In the last 10 years there has been a surge of UK government's interest in the teaching of thinking and problem-solving skills and schools are being asked to target development of these skills across the curriculum. Ofsted (1994) has identified that high-achieving students have been failing to reach the higher levels of the National Curriculum. It is suggested that the reason for this is that students cannot cope with the higher-order questions which need problem-solving approaches. Wallace and Adams (1993) argue that thinking skills are needed for all children, not just those who are the most intellectually able. They say that 'When all children are taught to use a range of thinking skills and problem solving skills and strategies, then all children's attainments rise,' and we would add 'including those with SLCN'.

## 4.3 Teaching thinking skills

The following elements are required in order to learn effective thinking and problem-solving skills:

- an adequate 'information base'; that is, a core vocabulary
- the 'tools'; that is, the vocabulary needed for thinking
- a structure which provides a scaffolding for thinking which is easy to remember and is transferable to other situations.

The most difficult aspect of planning to teach thinking skills is the context in which teaching takes place. These options include:

- separate thinking skills lessons
- within subject lessons such as science
- throughout the total curriculum.

Research indicates a roughly 50/50 split (Cotton, 1991) on whether separate lessons or 'infused programmes' (i.e. taught through the curriculum) are the most effective. Either way, time for delivery is needed from the curriculum for the skills to be successfully taught, understood and used. For students with SLCN, thinking skills are best taught initially through separate lessons in order for them to learn the language needed to understand the concepts that are involved. The introduction of any thinking skills programme for students with SLCN is also reliant on when they have acquired sufficient language to establish the 'adequate information base' to which De Bono refers in *The CoRT Thinking Programme* (1995). Provided that they have received support for their SLCN needs in key stages 1 and 2, this should have been achieved by the time they reach key stage 3/4. They will then also be more able to develop, understand and use the language for talking about thinking.

Research also indicates that thinking skills need to be taught over a period of time for them to be successful (Pogrow, 1988). For example, the CoRT programme spans 3 years.

The comments made by teachers about students not understanding language and not being able to express themselves are outlined in Chapters 2 and 6.

Equally, the poor ability to think through learning situations is commented upon:

- 'He couldn't plan a tea party.'
- 'She just doesn't seem to understand that there may be more than one answer to a problem.'

There are of course many reasons for the behaviour described, but the majority of the comments made were about students whose language needs were being addressed and yet they were still experiencing problems in a range of situations.

## 4.4 General guidelines for the teaching of thinking skills

### 4.1.1 The language

- Check the student's understanding of core and curriculum vocabulary.
- Pre-teach the language needed to think, talk and learn about thinking.
- Be ready to teach question forms since questioning is needed during the lessons.
- Categorize the language needed for thinking (e.g. feelings and hunches, facts and information).

### 4.4.2 The process

- Discuss what happens when you 'think' – give lots of examples and since it is an abstract concept, present the ideas visually and relate to personal/episodic memory. For example, 'You have pictures in your head about your holiday and can hear the conversations you had.'
- Help students to know and understand when they have been thinking. For example 'You have been thinking about whether it is best to travel to by train or car. You may have made notes or been talking to yourself in your head. You have been thinking.'
- Give model thinking lessons which are easy to understand.
- Begin by introducing non-emotional factual ideas/proposals not moral or ethical issues.
- Be aware that some kinds of thinking are more difficult to both teach and learn, especially thinking about thinking (meta-cognition).

### 4.4.3 Support for thinking

- Explain there are different kinds of thinking. Link these to visual representations.

- Use mind maps to help prioritization of information (e.g. into salient/not salient, helpful/not helpful).
- Help students verbalize their thinking by explaining that in some situations there may not be a 'right' answer.
- Translate into real-life situations wherever possible at first, otherwise some students may feel that learning to think is a waste of time. For example, 'Is it a good idea to climb lamp posts?' (This also links into social communication skills work and narrative structure).
- Use their real-life situations as a basis for some lessons, for example on disputes.
- Keep detailed records on progress.

### 4.4.4 Setting up a thinking skills programme

The prerequisites for introducing thinking skills to students have already been discussed and for students with SLCN a programme is best introduced in a limited way within a small group and then making links to aspects of the curriculum.

### 4.4.5 Choosing a programme

There are many thinking skills programmes available but two which have been found very useful for students with SLCN are De Bono's *Six Thinking Hats* (2000) and *The CoRT Thinking Programme* (De Bono, 1995). *Six Thinking Hats* is both visual and experiential and this provides scaffolding for learning. It links different types of thinking to different coloured hats and this programme was particularly helpful for Dylan.

 Case study: Dylan Year 10

Dylan had a long history of receptive language problems, but with support had made good progress. However, both staff in the facility and in his mainstream classes found him to be:
- very rigid in his approaches to problem solving
- poor at transferring his ideas to other situations
- poor at using his artistic skills which were a real strength, to think through situations
- becoming 'prickly' and frustrated when challenged about his work not being properly thought through.

When Dylan was asked by teachers in mainstream to stop and think about what he was doing, he would become very angry and say he was thinking very hard, but it didn't help. He was also becoming increasingly anxious about his future, even though he was constantly reassured he would receive help to make choices and decisions.

The teacher and therapist in the language facility decided to introduce a thinking skills programme using the 'Six Thinking Hats' approach, in order to help him and several other students. Three lessons a week were delivered first thing in the morning and these were continued throughout years 10 and 11.

Dylan learned:

- to understand and know when he was thinking
- when he needed to think (quite literally put his thinking hat on)
- 'how' to think
- what kind of thinking was most helpful in different situations
- how to apply different kinds of thinking to different learning situations in the curriculum.

He has decided to go to the local college to study art and design and is now quite happy and convinced this is the right path for him to be following.

## Points to remember

- Language is a key tool in the development of thinking skills.
- There are many different ways of thinking and they can be taught.
- Students with SLCN need to have thinking skills taught as a specific skill and then generalized into the content of the curriculum.
- Visual support is effective in teaching thinking skills to students with SLCN.

# 5

# Clear About Speech

**Chapter Objectives**

> To explain the difference between an articulation difficulty and a phonological difficulty
> To outline the impact that phonological difficulties have on the development of phonological awareness and literacy
> To discuss the most commonly seen developmental/neurological conditions in which speech is likely to be impaired
> To provide strategies to support students with speech difficulties in class

## 5.1 Speech difficulties

Poor intelligibility of spoken language is most obvious to the listener and in fact many people, inaccurately, equate speech difficulties with SLCN. So what exactly do we mean by 'speech difficulties'? Teachers, when asked about a child's speech problem, will usually make a comment such as 'He can't say his sounds and is very difficult to understand.' A child's speech may be unintelligible because sounds, both consonants and vowels, are omitted, substituted or distorted. However, the problem may not just be at the sound production level. There may be other accompanying problems of voice control and resonance. These other aspects of speech (volume, intonation, stress patterns, etc.) are referred to collectively as 'prosody' and when impaired, interfere significantly with intelligibility and also with conveying meaning.

There are many reasons why a student may be unable to articulate sounds correctly:

- They may have a physical difficulty with the structure of their mouth, such as cleft lip and palate.
- They may have a neurological impairment affecting the movements of the muscles of their mouth, throat and chest, such as found in children with the condition cerebral palsy.

- They may have a syndrome (e.g. Down's syndrome) in which difficulties of speech are a feature.
- They may have a sensory impairment (e.g. deafness).
- They may have the condition developmental verbal dyspraxia (DVD) which affects the planning, organization and sequencing of speech sounds for words and for words into sentences.
- They may come from a multilingual background where they are learning differing speech sounds systems at the same time.

Students with speech problems have difficulty in actually making the speech sounds, in the right place in their mouths, in the right manner, at the right time and with the correct balance of those aspects of speech we call prosody (speed, intonation, etc.). This kind of problem is referred to as an 'articulatory difficulty'.

With some students, however, there is no obvious cause for their lack of intelligibility. Speech and language therapists are often asked by concerned parents and professionals why it is that in the absence of any obvious disability, young children cannot articulate their language. There is so far no clear answer for this, although research is ongoing.

The students who have no obvious physical cause for their lack of intelligibility may have difficulties with the sound system itself: phonological problems. They use a restricted number of sounds in their speech, which are not sufficient to express meaning clearly. It appears that it is their **understanding and use of the system of speech sounds** that is affected. Consequently, this type of speech difficulty is often described as a 'phonological difficulty'. There are rules to be understood regarding the ways in which sounds are organized in language, to convey differences of meaning. These students have problems with learning the rules.

The distinction between an articulation difficulty and a phonological difficulty is important since it reflects how speech and language therapists interpret speech difficulties and guides them towards the most appropriate approach to take for intervention. Also, a significant body of research indicates that early speech difficulties described as phonological in origin link to later problems with literacy.

## 5.2 Persisting speech difficulties in students aged 11 to 19

### 5.2.1 Phonological difficulties

The distinction has already been made between those students who have problems with articulation and those who have problems with phonology. It is unusual for children with phonological difficulties to still be unintelligible at key stages 3 and 4, assuming they have received sufficient and timely intervention. Persisting problems are usually evident in more subtle ways:

- Learning new and complex words. They do not easily store them with the correct speech sound patterns – referred to as 'phonological representations'. Hence when they need to say the word, it is reproduced in the same incorrect way that they have stored it away.
- Saying difficult words they already know.
- Word retrieval difficulties.
- All of the above plus poor knowledge of word boundaries which leads to unclear connected speech.
- Poor phonological awareness.

The term 'phonological awareness' refers to the set of skills which enables us to analyze the words we hear and say (Layton *et al.*, 1997). This set of skills enables us to:

- identify words as separate units when in sentences
- understand and use rhyme
- identify and produce syllables in words
- identify and produce first sounds in words (onset)
- identify and produce the rest of the word (rime)
- to segment and blend sounds in words.

The acquisition of this complex set of skills is totally dependent on a child first having an excellent knowledge of phonology; that is, the understanding and use of the system of speech sounds.

A substantial body of evidence has shown that the early development of these skills is pivotal to the later skills of reading and spelling (Bradley and Bryant, 1985; Goswami, 1996; and Snowling and Stackhouse, 1996). Children with early phonological difficulties are 'at risk' for literacy problems and may well need support for phonological awareness well into secondary school, even though in theory they should by then have all the fundamental skills for reading and spelling.

It has been estimated that 80% of students who are identified as dyslexic have a core problem with phonology. Their weak phonological memories and their poor understanding of the phonological rules for language make it hard for them to access a phonic approach to reading or spelling. This is why they respond best to multi-sensory approaches.

Although their difficulties with intelligibility may be residual and quite minor by key stage 3, this group of students may have written language skills so fragile that their access to the curriculum is severely restricted:

- They cannot decode new subject-specific vocabulary.
- They confuse visually similar words.
- They have reading that is so laboured and effortful that they read less and understand little of what they have read.
- Their writing is characterized by bizarre spelling.
- Their written contribution is poor, even compared with their oral contributions.
- Their study skills are poor.
- They may be reluctant to start writing tasks or to persevere with writing tasks, which can have behavioural consequences.

## 5.2.2 Articulatory difficulties

The most obvious speech difficulties will be articulatory in origin and have a well-defined cause.

### 5.2.2.1 Cleft lip and palate

Children born with cleft lip and palate nowadays are usually operated on in the first few months of life. The process of acquiring intelligible speech for those with the most complex clefts can take many years, continuing into secondary school. Children with cleft lip and palate frequently suffer from conductive hearing loss, a common complication of the condition.

### 5.2.2.2 Hearing impairment

There are two main types of hearing loss: conductive and sensori-neural. It is unusual for a conductive hearing loss to persist into key stages 3 and 4, but its effects on early speech development may have had an impact on literacy. More commonly found at this stage are students with a sensori-neural hearing impairment. Nowadays, amplification in the form of new technology hearing aids, has significantly improved the chances of a child being able to cope in a regular mainstream school.

### 5.2.2.3 Neurological impairment

This is an umbrella term, encompassing many types of brain injury acquired through injury or illness. Speech difficulties of neurological origin are referred to as 'dysarthrias' (e.g. students with 'cerebral palsy' have speech which is typically dysarthric). Different students have different degrees of difficulty, but all will have some of the following to a greater or lesser degree:

- slurred articulation caused by difficulties of motor co-ordination
- tense and staccato speech delivery due to increased muscle tone
- poor quality of voice owing to poor muscle and breath control
- poor lip posture and swallowing for saliva control due to poor muscle tone and co-ordination of the muscles used for swallowing.

Students with this type of speech difficulty can be supported by more general strategies in school:

- be given time to 'have their say'
- have PE differentiated to enable them to participate to improve balance and co-ordination
- participate in out of school classes such as yoga to improve relaxation, co-ordination and breathing
- participate in singing/choir to improve pace and timing with breathing for 'sung speech'
- when reading out loud in regular class or drama class, draw attention to breathing so that meaning is not compromised
- use reading to practice any specific sounds that are being targeted by the speech and language therapist
- encourage 'total' communication, as this supports verbal communication and takes the pressure off it, allowing the student to relax and produce 'best' speech.

## 5.3 Dyspraxia or developmental co-ordination disorder (DCD)

Both of these terms are now used to describe the same condition, although different practitioners will certainly have different ideas on how they are understood.

For the majority of children, their verbal dyspraxic difficulties will have resolved by key stages 3 and 4. However, for some there may be continuing problems which are described on the website. These difficulties with spoken  language may have an impact on their written language in key stages 3 and 4.

Many students with DCD also experience difficulties with understanding and using the speech sound system. Therefore, as well as the strategies used with Edgar, they may benefit from specific strategies to:

- improve phonological awareness
- support literacy
- support spelling.

Case study: Edgar, Year 7

Edgar was not always intelligible to those who did not know him. He was still experiencing problems with:

- the sounds 's', 'r', 'y', 'sh' and 'ch'
- many vowel sounds were still distorted
- many aspects of prosody
- inconsistent nasality
- pausing in the right places in a sentence when speaking.

Unlike many students of his age with DCD, Edgar's language was excellent and when teachers and peers commented on how difficult he was to understand, Edgar became very annoyed with them all. Edgar had come from a supportive and nurturing school where staff and children had known him for a long time and were able to understand his speech.

It was suggested that the TA support the therapy programme on a daily basis and also encourage him to:

- Think through what he was going to say and rehearse it in his head in order to get the pauses correct – if necessary, have a book of 'What I say everyday' and write down how each part of the 'script' should be said.
- Be aware of the speed of his speech and check that others were understanding him.
- Write down new key curriculum words in his books and learn them correctly. If necessary, take them to therapy to practice with the therapist.
- When learning these new long and complex words, use syllable boxes to help learn syllable structure of the words.
- Join the choir to help his understanding of rhythm and intonation.

## 5.4 Syndromes

There are many children in mainstream school who have different syndromes. It is not within the remit of this book to go into detail with these as there are literally hundreds identified. Perhaps the most common syndrome seen in mainstream school is Down's syndrome. There are many typical features of this syndrome, including delay/disorder of speech and language.

Speech difficulties are usually as follows, with some or all of the features described:

- poor articulation
- poor phonology
- reduced muscle tone in the tongue and other speech organs which can also cause drooling, mouth breathing and feeding difficulties
- speech can be monotonous (i.e. aspects of prosody can be affected)
- hearing impairment is common, usually conductive.

The case study of Eric is an example of how a student with Down's syndrome may be supported in secondary school.

This chapter has dealt with how we make the speech and sounds of our language. For students to continue to experience speech difficulty at secondary school is a huge disability and although not as common as some other aspects of SEN, the results are just as destructive.

 Case study: Eric, Year 10

Eric had Down's syndrome and had received speech and language therapy from an early age. By the time he reached secondary school Eric was mostly intelligible to those who knew him and his language skills had improved so much that the staff in school only needed advice on how best to deal with those remaining difficulties of comprehension and expression. However, he continued to need ongoing help with his speech, which was characterized by the following:
- imprecise pronunciation of 's', 'r', 'ch', 'sh', 'l' and 'y'
- poor production of polysyllabic words
- monotonous speech
- speech that was too fast and too loud.

Eric worked very hard on his speech sounds and, although by year 10 they were not perfect, they were precise enough to be understood, especially as he had received a great deal of help for other aspects of his speech. The school worked with speech and language therapists by providing:
- a TA to follow up a speech programme
- extra time in music to help with rhythm, pitch, intonation
- a social communication skills group for learning and using the protocols of conversation (i.e. speed, volume and best articulation).

Points to remember

- Speech difficulties that persist in key stages 3 and 4 and are particularly disabling for the student.
- Speech difficulties can be caused by a variety of developmental, neurological and sensory problems.
- Persisting phonological problems impact significantly on the development of reading and spelling.
- A variety of different strategies is needed to support different types of speech difficulty. With some students these may be provided by a speech and language therapist but for most students support will be provided in the context of the curriculum by education staff.

6

# Talking Language

> **Chapter Objectives**
>
> > **To help teachers recognize expressive language difficulties from the responses of their students**
> > **To alert teachers to the social consequences of not being able to communicateeffectively**
> > **To provide strategies to support students in the classroom**
> > **To present strategies to address the difficulties of individual students**

## 6.1 Recognizing expressive language difficulties

In Chapter 5, 'Clear About Speech', the difficulties that students may still experience with intelligibility were discussed. For most students at secondary school any residual speech problems may only be apparent when the student is under stress or excited. Nevertheless, some individuals may struggle to express their needs and ideas because of expressive language problems. The case study of Frank illustrates some of the frustrations that they might experience. When these students do make a contribution to class discussions or attempt to answer a question, the teacher may become aware of the following:

- They have to wait for the answer while the student attempts to organize how he will express an idea and select the appropriate vocabulary. This can disrupt the 'flow' of an exchange and another member of the class will often have chipped in with the response before the target student makes his contribution.
- Once the student has started to speak, he often pauses in mid-sentence and/or repeats what he has just said (mazing) while he organizes the next part of the utterance.

- The student seems to struggle to find the words he needs or substitute words that sound the same or have a similar meaning to the target word. These are signs of word-finding problems, which were discussed in detail in Chapter 3.
- The student may show word order problems in a sentence and this may be reflected in their written work at a sentence level or at the level of sequencing ideas.

Teachers might say:

- 'He speaks very slowly.'
- 'He can't seem to find the words.'

Students who are uncertain about their ability to communicate effectively may, understandably, have acquired a reluctance to attempt to communicate. This may be more obvious in some settings than others; for example, with adults, with peers or in a group. Teachers may become aware that the student is reluctant to volunteer information, respond to questions or join in class discussions. When group work takes place the student may be an observer rather than a participator. The pressure to talk may exacerbate an existing dysfluency which is potentially very embarrassing for the student. A refusal to respond may be interpreted as defiance rather than a difficulty with communication so that many of these students are excluded from school, as discussed in Chapter 8, 'Talking Behaviour'. Often students with expressive language problems try to keep their verbal contribution to a minimum so that they may present as monosyllabic, telegrammatic or even rude (like Brenda). They are not able to talk themselves out of trouble, make excuses, explain misunderstandings or justify their behaviour to others.

 Case study: Frank, Year 8

Frank had a history of SLI and his language profile indicated that his expressive language skills were the main area of concern. He was referred to the Educational Psychology Services in year 8 at the request of his mother who was concerned about:

- slow progress with literacy skills
- high levels of anxiety about changes of routine and his work
- destructive behaviour at home when he was anxious and stressed.

Frank was interviewed on two occasions. At the first meeting he showed high levels of anxiety and associated pragmatic difficulties which were not present at the second interview when he was more relaxed. When he was anxious he:

- kept his head down and seldom made eye contact

- steered the topic of conversation back to familiar subjects at any opportunity
- asked anxiety-related questions.

Assessment indicated that he found it hard to construct a coherent narrative, even when describing a recent event that he had experienced: an accident on his bike. He was able to sequence the main events but

- did not cue in the listener by making clear who was involved, when and where
- did not use full sentences, pronouns or connectors to link the sequence of ideas
- failed to give sufficient detail of key points so that the listener had to ask supplementary questions to clarify what had really happened.

Frank was able to identify his problems with explaining what he wanted to say as 'Know it in my head; can't say it.' Further assessment indicated that he had limited word knowledge in association with more specific word-finding problems for which he used the strategy of circum-locution; for example, target word 'gills' (of a fish): 'things to breathe'.

Frank's difficulties with expressive language caused him frustration and affected his confidence as a communicator. He had vented his frus-trations at home by being destructive ('smashing things up' – mother) but his behaviour in school was not an issue in year 8.

Frank found it hard to express himself verbally and so constructing what he wanted to say in the written form presented significant problems in the classroom setting. Frank perceived that he was struggling with the year 8 curriculum and his self-esteem as a learner was low so that he expected to fail when any new activity was introduced. He clearly expected to 'fail' in year 9.

Teachers might say:

- 'He never says anything.'
- 'He's surly, disaffected – a typical teenager.'
- 'He's just shy.'

A few students who present with elective/selective mutism may have underlying expressive language problems. Some students may be labelled as a liar because of the strategies that they have adopted to manage their expressive problems:

- They have learned that a positive 'yes' response is usually expected and pleases the listener. A simple 'yes' is often easier than attempting to explain what really happened. Sometimes, however, 'yes' is not the appropriate option.

- In a group setting it may be easier to repeat what someone else has said rather than attempt to express one's own ideas or relate personal experiences. This 'copying' may be perceived as negative by the group.

Students may appear to be quite verbally competent, especially in social situations, but their attempts at more formal language indicates problems with the use of the abstract, decontextualized language that is expected in the classroom (Cummins, 1986). Specific problems may be noticed in the following areas:

- The recall of events in a logical sequence (e.g. describing an experiment, talking about a school trip).
- Using language to explain ideas or define words: this is a complex meta-linguistic skill. Typically, the student may relate a personal anecdote to illustrate a concept such as 'lying' rather than discussing the concepts of trust or truth.

Some responses by the students may reveal underlying difficulties with understanding (i.e. receptive language problems). Teachers may notice problems with the following:

- Getting the main idea of an explanation or discussion.
- Giving off-target responses to questions which indicates that they have only responded to part of the message or only to key words in what has been said. Under some circumstances this type of response can appear defiant or odd enough to 'set the others off by making silly remarks'.

Teacher: 'Where is Wednesday night's maths homework?'

Student: 'Gran came Wednesday.'

Students who experience difficulties with expressive language are at risk of social exclusion and the research evidence indicates that this process may begin even before children start school (Hadley and Rice, 1991). Over time, their ability to communicate may improve but the pattern of difficult social relationships may continue into adolescence unless the problems are addressed. Davis *et al.* (1991), in a study which compared the skills of delinquent and non-delinquent boys, found that the former showed a reduced capacity to engage in conversational interactions. Their limited communication skills had an impact on their relationships with other people.

Some students who have SLI may not have obvious difficulties in a social context: their basic social interactions appear to be competent (BICS). However, Nelson (1981) found that many of these students have developed conversational scripts that they are able to use in a social context. Their scripts are based on everyday knowledge of situations and serve the person well in familiar situations. The scripts are in place for social greetings and familiar exchanges and allow the person to 'pass' socially and mask their underlying difficulties. The social scripts break down in unfamiliar situations and do not equip the individual to access the more abstract, decontextualized language which is the main medium for teaching and learning in the classroom.

Teachers may notice the following:

- Social isolation with few friends.
- A reduced participation in work groups and social activities.
- Distress in response to verbal teasing or banter because they do not have the verbal skills to respond in kind, like Brenda.
- A physical response to social situations because they find it hard to explain their actions, negotiate or solve disputes verbally. They may quickly acquire a reputation for aggressive behaviour, like Andy.
- Signs of frustration and/or high levels of anxiety. Students often find themselves in situations to which they are unable to respond appropriately. The fear of being unable to respond may generate anxious vigilance even in relatively relaxed settings.

The descriptions of behaviour from teachers include:

- 'They don't choose him as a partner for group work.'
- 'He is very aggressive, thumps for no reason.'
- 'Other students don't like him.'

## 6.2 Classroom strategies to support students with expressive language problems

Some effective strategies may be managed as part of the lesson routine. These would include:

- the careful use of questioning – for some students closed questions or forced alternatives may be the most effective way of including them
- allowing extra time for the student to organize the language in order to reply to a question
- scaffolding questions to support longer explanations or contributions by the student.

The students may find it difficult to participate in group activities because the skills that people need in order to operate as a member of a group are demanding on language:

- a willingness to participate
- listening to the contribution of other group members

- understanding (getting the main ideas) and considering the contributions of others
- stating ideas clearly
- negotiation skills
- a range of pragmatic skills: verbal and non-verbal.

It is helpful if teachers can give some thought to group allocation for students with SLCN:

- choice of partners or group members
- the allocation of roles to group members to ensure that the student with expressive language problems has a role that they can fulfil and experience success
- the allocation of roles to give opportunities for the student with expressive problems to demonstrate non-verbal strengths in the group and in front of the whole class
- paired working or small groups to give the students the chance to prepare and practice the delivery of 'model' answers, or how to report on their work.

At times when there is additional support in the lesson, TAs may work with individuals or small groups of students to:

- provide opportunities for discussion in the safe context of a small group with an adult facilitator
- pre-prepare
  - topic vocabulary with a focus on new words and concepts together with common use words that have an alternative meaning in the context of the subject/topic (discussed in more detail in Chapter 2)
  - presentations
  - model answers in a small group setting (the teacher and TA agree in advance what question(s) the student will be asked in the whole class setting).

It is important that all subject teachers are aware of students who have expressive language difficulties so that they can avoid putting the student under pressure to explain situations or account for their behaviour. If the student needs to give an explanation, it is important to support them with the use of structured questions. The framework of the narrative approach (Chapter 2) has been shown to be helpful in this context, particularly once the 'heat' of the moment is past and the student is calm. Teachers should always try to avoid calling to account students with expressive language problems in a public setting as this may provoke a hostile reaction if the student is already in a high state of arousal.

Young offenders who were studied by Bryan (2004) reported that they used violence when they found it difficult to communicate and make their needs known. They also responded with aggression when they were teased because they were unskilled at verbal forms of bantering defence.

Students who have expressive language impairment are likely to be vulnerable during the less structured times of the school day because of the barriers to social inclusion that were discussed earlier in the chapter. They are vulnerable to teasing and verbal bullying and, because they are not able to respond verbally, may resort to a physical response. It is, therefore, appropriate to consider alternative arrangements at lunch or break times. Many secondary schools do have a 'haven' for vulnerable students who are at risk during unstructured times. Peer support through mentor systems or a circle of friends have proved helpful for some students. It is important to involve the students in discussions about what situations they find stressful and the strategies that would be acceptable to them.

## 6.3   Strategies to support individual students with expressive language problems

In Chapter 2, Figure 2.1 illustrated the component skills necessary in order to understand narrative – what someone is saying. Figure 6.1 illustrates the component skills that are required to construct a message. These skills are first developed in an oral context before they transfer to the written context. Teachers rarely get the opportunity to have extended conversations with their students and so it is usually through written texts that the difficulties with the organization of expressive language are noticed. In conversation, problems with sequencing and salience may be apparent so that the listener rapidly becomes confused as they try to get the gist of what is being said. During a conversation about a teacher-led topic, it may be possible to identify a range of features:

- Conversations are difficult to follow as the student appears to have no clear understanding of what should be said first/next/last in order to make the message clear.
- The student does not seem to find it easy to identify the main ideas or the salient information, a skill pivotal to academic success.
- The student does not filter out the irrelevant information in conversation or learning situations – appears to 'waffle'.
- The student does not 'set the scene', supply the background information that is necessary in order for the listener to understand the message.

The remainder of the chapter will focus on the components of the model.

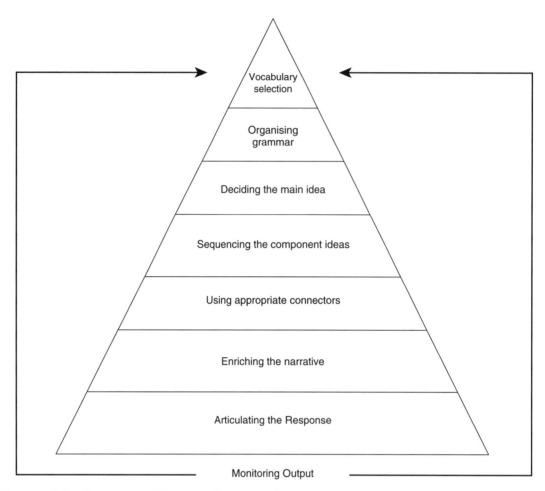

**Figure 6.1**  To express ideas: spoken or written.

### 6.3.1 Vocabulary knowledge

In Chapter 2 some strategies for teaching new vocabulary in ways that support students with SLCN were introduced and the acquisition of receptive vocabulary – the words that are understood – precedes the ability to use those words. Once a store of receptive vocabulary has been built up for both common use and subject specific words, students may still struggle to make an appropriate choice of words and to retrieve words from their lexicon. How to recognize difficulties with retrieval were discussed in Chapter 3.

 In this chapter the focus is on the specific strategies to address word retrieval problems. Students can be taught specific strategies to aid word retrieval and research has shown that they benefit most from an approach combining the following, plus the use of natural gesture or signing:

- Accessing the word by the appropriate meaning (semantic)
- Accessing the grammatical information; for example, what group of words does it fit into (i.e. the name of something (noun), an action (verb), a descriptive word (adjective))?

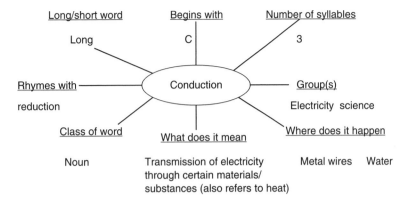

**Figure 6.2**  Adding more information.

- Accessing the phonological information; for example,
  - what sound it starts with
  - what it rhymes with/sounds like
  - how many syllables it has.

Students can be encouraged to sort key vocabulary words according to one of the above features or make a 'category' dictionary for any new vocabulary that has to be learnt. Category dictionaries are also very useful for learning new vocabulary and assisting word retrieval. The dictionary contains category pages and the categories can be colour coded, another feature to assist recall (e.g. science = blue, maths = red, etc.). Other information can then be added using the various features already outlined (semantic, grammatical, phonological) (Figure 6.2).

### 6.3.2 Use of a range of grammatical structures

#### 6.3.2.1 Support for developing grammar

Students who have expressive language problems may be able to appear grammatically competent during casual social exchanges but their written work may reveal underlying difficulties with the more sophisticated aspects of grammar which are needed in order to access the curriculum. The following section identifies the areas of grammar that may still present problems at secondary school and offers some ideas about how to support these students.

#### 6.3.2.2 Teaching grammatical structures

Visual coding is a useful way to help children with SLCN to learn aspects of grammar. There are several systems available including shape coding

(Ebbels, 2007) and colour coding. The most common areas of difficulty include:

### 6.3.2.2.1 Irregular plural nouns

- These need to be learned and can be taught through games such as 'spot the wrong word' – ask the student to tell you whether the word that has been said sounds right or wrong when you make it into a plural (e.g. cats, dogs, houses, mans, tables).
- Teach a targeted number of irregular plurals by connecting them to the singular nouns (e.g. man – men, mouse – mice, etc.).
- Next, mix these with regular pairs for a 'pairs matching' game.

### 6.3.2.2.2 Irregular past verb tense

- Make sure that the student understands the regular rule (i.e. 'ed' ending).
- Compile a list of commonly used irregular verbs.

### 6.3.2.2.3 Negation

The basics of negation have been acquired by the time most students reach secondary school, for example

- The development of '... n't' with more complex verbs.
- With passive form of the verb – 'The child wasn't being protected with the use of a seat belt.'
- The use of double negatives for emphasis (e.g. 'You couldn't **not** want to please her.')

These are best taught explicitly through the medium of written language supported by visuals, using a small-steps approach (e.g. initially supply possible answers for an exercise).

### 6.3.2.2.4 Marking reference

Pronouns are frequently difficult to understand as they replace a noun and are relative. 'You' refers to the listener in a verbal interaction, but 'you' then changes as the listener becomes the speaker.

- Students need to understand that pronouns *replace* nouns:
- Give choices for one pronoun in a sentence; for example, _____ caught the bus (the lady/he/she)
  - Using icons to represent he/she may help.
  - He/she can also refer back to an individual in the sentence or in a previous sentence. 'Mark went out to catch the 4 o'clock bus. He missed it and waited for another 10 minutes.' 'He' refers to 'Mark'. This relationship needs explaining.
- Next describe a story where only pronouns are used (e.g. 'I got up this morning, but he went there first so I went downstairs to eat it because she had been calling me and we were going to be late.') Proper nouns and pronouns all need to be used to ensure clarity of meaning.

### 6.3.2.2.5 Conjunctions

These are simply described as 'joining' words; that is, words that join one sentence to another (e.g. 'He got up. He washed his hands' becomes 'He got up **and** he washed his hands.')

Although 'and' is the most common conjunction and, therefore, the assumption would be that it is the simplest, it can in fact perform a variety of different functions. Since pupils with SLCN tend to continue using 'and' as a connector to the exclusion of all others, its various functions can be used to support understanding and use of more complex connectors as follows:

- consequence or result of an action or event; for example, 'She was thirsty **and** drank some water' - meaning **therefore** or **so**
- for a sequential event; for example, 'I got up **and** I got washed.' – meaning **then**
- for a conditional relationship; for example, 'You do my hair **and** I'll do your nails' – meaning if you do *x* then I'll do *y*
- for a pure addition; for example, 'She has a blue dress **and** she has new shoes.' – meaning **also**.

### 6.3.2.2.6 Temporal connections

The phrase 'and then' can be used to introduce 'when', 'before', 'while', 'until' and 'after', since as students need to understand these and words associated with time. For most students with SLCN, 'time' is a difficult concept.

### 6.3.2.2.7 Causal connections

'And' can be used to make causal connections (see previously) where 'and' means 'so'. Other causal words include 'because', '(in order) to' and 'so that'.

### 6.3.2.2.8 Teaching question forms

The first question form that children learn and use is by making their voices go up at the end of a phrase (inflection); for example, 'Mummy come?' meaning 'Are you coming now mummy?', 'Will you come with me mummy?' and so on. The next form of questioning is by the use of question words. For example, 'when' refers to time and 'why' refers to reason.

Not all students will be able to understand and/or use these basic question forms when they transfer to secondary school. Later, increasingly complex question forms begin to emerge which rely on more sophisticated grammar. Examples of these are as follows:

- tag questions: 'I'm finished, aren't I?'
- question forms using: progressive present, past and future tense verbs
- question forms using perfect present, past and future tense verbs

- question forms using perfect, progressive, present, past and future tense verbs
- question forms using modal auxiliary verbs (e.g. May I sit here?)
- question forms using the passive voice
- negative questions (e.g. 'Doesn't he have a ticket?').

For more information please refer to Toomey (1994).

There are many opportunities within the day to learn and practice questioning. For example, in tutor time ('How are you?', 'Are you better?', 'When is assembly?').

There are other opportunities to teach more complex grammatical forms; for example, teachers frequently ask students 'Have you been talking?' or 'What do you think will happen if you don't do your homework?' Structured activities to teach the more sophisticated and complex question forms include role play and discussion of texts.

The discussion about expressive language has highlighted the difficulties that some students may experience with sharing their thoughts, ideas and experiences, even if their speech is intelligible. By the time these students reach key stage 3, they may have developed strategies to disguise their problems. Staff need to be aware of the 'markers' for expressive language problems which might explain what at first sight appear to be difficulties with behaviour or social interaction.

## Points to remember

- Students may speak clearly but still experience problems with expressive language: organizing what they want to say.
- Expressive language problems may affect how students respond and participate in the classroom.
- Students who have expressive language problems may need support to develop social relationships and these students are particularly at risk for developing behaviour problems at secondary school.
- Students who have expressive language problems may be particularly vulnerable during the unstructured times of the school day.
- Teachers seldom have the opportunity for extended conversations with their students and so expressive language difficulties may first be picked up through their written language.

# 7

# Socially Speaking

**Chapter Objectives**

> To explain the key features of pragmatic difficulties and how they may affect students socially and in the classroom
> To provide a framework for working with social skills at secondary school:
>   > how to plan a social skills group
>   > how to involve parents and students
>   > solutions to practical issues
>   > session planning
>   > techniques which are used in group sessions
> Sample session plans are presented on the website for guidance
> The Practice Pack on the website gives sample proformas for group planning

## 7.1 Introduction

Human beings from their earliest hours spend time interacting with other people. The current resurgence of interest in the role of attachment in development emphasizes the importance of these early encounters in promoting individual development and emotional wellbeing (Gerhardt, 2004). Communication, at first non-verbal but later verbal, is of prime importance in establishing social relationships. For children who are unable to communicate verbally their opportunities to participate in satisfying interactions and form good relationships are reduced. The implications of this for their subsequent behaviour are discussed in detail in Chapter 8, 'Talking Behaviour'.

This chapter is concerned with the way in which students are able to use their language in order to communicate effectively. Students may have an adequate understanding of what is said to them (receptive language) and be able to execute an utterance that can be understood by others (expressive language) but still find it hard to communicate – to make the connection with another person in terms of what they say or how they say it.

Pragmatics is the term given to the study of the functions and purposes for which language is used (the **why** of communication) and the way in which we react to what others say and deliver our message (the **how** of communication) (see Figure 7.1).

The 'why' aspect relates to the goal or intention of language use; for example, to seek information, to comment and to contradict.

The functions and purposes for which we use language extend with the development of our language. Locke (1984) identifies eight functions which are achieved by key stage 2 and by key stage 3 we might add functions such as debating, negotiating and all the aspects of language which are described in Chapter 4, 'Thinking Language'.

It is the 'how' aspect of pragmatics that has attracted the most attention in recent years, primarily because this is the area of language use that is associated strongly with autistic spectrum disorders. However, students who experience difficulties with speech and language may also show difficulties with 'how' they communicate.

- A child who has reduced intelligibility because of phonological problems may look down and avoid eye contact, so that people don't ask him

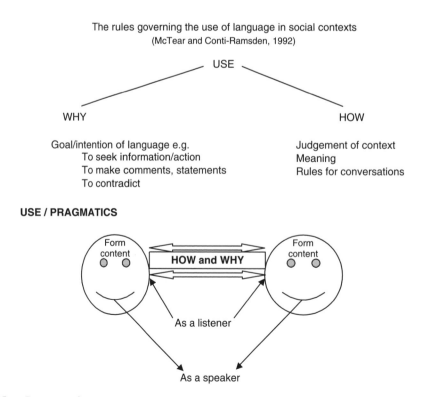

**Figure 7.1** Pragmatics.

questions, but ask the child sitting next to him. (Adults do the same at conferences/courses when we ask for volunteers for role play.) It is a strategy that makes sense.

- A child with significant receptive problems may equally avoid social encounters and prefer to sit alone at a table for lunch to avoid the usual conversational exchanges or prefer to play alone. Such children may appear to have 'autistic features' when the behaviour is viewed out of context.

These complexities are addressed in more detail in Chapter 9, 'Assessing Speech and Language'.

It is the long-held view of the authors that pragmatic problems may be secondary to speech and language impairment and are not exclusive to autistic spectrum disorders. This was also the consensus view of speakers at the 2007 Afasic Conference.

The remainder of this chapter will focus on the identification of pragmatic difficulties and the role of social skills training in supporting students to develop more successful ways of interacting with others.

## 7.2 The identification of pragmatic difficulties

In the classroom students who have pragmatic difficulties may present as rather 'odd' or even challenging. Descriptions of their behaviour from subject teachers might include:

- 'He doesn't know when to stop talking.'
- 'He will just say anything and is often quite rude.'
- 'He keeps shouting out and disturbing the other students.'
- 'He pesters me with questions even when he can see I am talking to another student.'
- 'He will challenge what I say to the group.'

The use of language in terms of the Lahey and Bloom (1988) model was one of the last aspects of language to be analyzed in a systematic way. A smooth communication exchange appears so effortless that it has proved hard to break the skilled performance down into its component parts and the assessment tools that are available are essentially qualitative. However, it is possible to identify key components of a communication exchange that may be difficult for students who experience pragmatic problems:

- How and when to initiate a conversation: choosing the moment and selecting an appropriate form of words to start the exchange.

• Taking into account what the listener needs to know in order to cue them in about the topic (not: 'It was crowded'; but: 'When we went shopping on Saturday ...').

The cueing in process also needs to take into account the listener's prior knowledge of the topic and we all use our own professional jargon; for example, key stage 3, wave 3, as a shortcut to communication but the conversation would not necessarily be accessible to an outsider:

• The perception that the speaker does not know when to stop talking may reflect confusion about when they have said enough to have answered the question and how much detail it is appropriate to give in that particular context.
• The rules of turn taking in a conversation may be violated by one person dominating the exchange and effectively giving a monologue.
• An awareness of the reciprocal nature of a conversation needs to also be at a deeper level than following turn-taking conventions. Each person needs to be able to take on the role of speaker and listener and to monitor the needs of their conversational partner. Are they still interested? Do they want to have to go?
• The ability to maintain a topic of conversation without going off at a tangent. The rules governing how conversations evolve and advance are particularly subtle. When we meet a new person we may be conscious of the exploring and probing that goes on in order to establish a topic that appears to be of mutual interest.
• In the classroom knowing when it is appropriate to talk and when to be quiet is a particularly important skill.
• To avoid being seen as rude or over-familiar in a social exchange, it is necessary to make language choices. We need to modify what we say and how we say it in order to address our audience appropriately. Even then we might not use the same form of address to a person in different contexts; for example when your mother is also your science teacher.
• The art of ending a conversation without appearing abrupt or rude is a final important skill. The form of words that is used, together with the social conventions such as smiles or hand shakes are all important for negotiating a successful end to an encounter which satisfies both participants. Reading and responding to the cues that the other person wishes to end the exchange may be particularly hard for students who experience pragmatic problems.

The subtleties of a conversational exchange involve not only the verbal component but also the non-verbal components of language use. Students need to be adept at both 'reading' and providing non-verbal cues. As early as 1972, Mehrabian wrote that 93% of the information that is transmitted from person to person is non-verbal. We are constantly encoding the non-verbal messages and assessing their congruity with the verbal message.

Skilled and/or professional communicators try to ensure that their body language supports the verbal message. Non-verbal cues also play an important role in regulating conversational exchanges such as turn taking or ending the conversation appropriately. Bridging between the verbal and non-verbal skills that govern a successful, or unsuccessful, exchange are the paralinguistic skills such as the rate, volume and prosodic features of our speech. The complexity of a successful conversation is represented in Figure 7.2.

The pragmatic aspects of language may be seen as even more complex and subtle than understanding a message: receptive language (Figure 2.1) or planning a message: expressive language (Figure 6.1). Skill communicators are constantly adapting, both what they say and how they say it according to the feedback that they receive from their 'audience'.

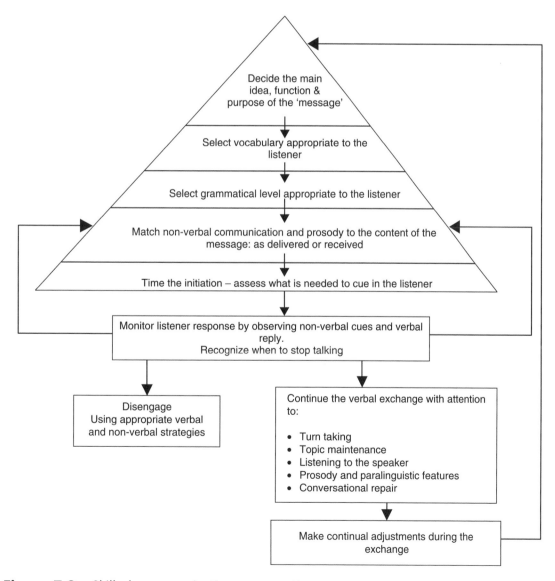

**Figure 7.2**  Skilled communication: pragmatics.

Students who have SLCN may have difficulties with all or some of the aspects of pragmatics that have been discussed. However, as documented in the cases of Alice and Brenda some of these students have such strong social, pragmatic skills that they manage to disguise their receptive language problems all too effectively.

The social skills that we have come to recognize in everyday life, and that are a necessary component of emotional literacy, are predominantly the skills of effective communication. Social skills as a 'skill set' were first identified and analyzed by Argyle (1982) who described them as:

- behaviours that were learned by observation and experience
- behaviours that were overt and observable by others.

There followed a proliferation of lists of behaviours that were identified as components of social skill (e.g. eye contact, proxemics, etc.). Two key messages emerge that are useful for practitioners working to support students:

- Social skills are learned and, therefore, can be taught.
- It is important to focus on the student and identify the social skills that they need to learn rather than taking an unfocused, generic approach.

## 7.3 Working with social skills in secondary school

The aim of promoting social skills in the secondary setting is to help individuals to interact more skilfully according to the social expectations of the cultural context; for example, in the classroom, playground or at home. Teaching social skills can improve both the quality and quantity of social interactions for people who have experienced difficulties. A prerequisite to setting up a social skills group is to obtain the support of the senior management team in the school as there are organizational issues that will need to be addressed such as:

- timetabling the sessions
- release of staff for training
- release of staff for planning and leading the groups
- prioritizing social skills within the curriculum.

The support of the wider staff team will need to be engaged through awareness-raising about the importance of social skills training in promoting positive behaviour and emotional literacy. Subject teachers may be quite sensitive about students missing their lessons unless they are convinced that the training is a priority for the students. It is possible to run a pilot study in a school to provide the evidence for the effectiveness of social skills training in changing behaviour in the classroom. Details of the pilot study carried out in one secondary school can be found on the website.

## 7.4 Planning a social skills group

### 7.4.1 Selection of students

The identification of potential group members may depend on the priorities within the school. In the pilot study the decision had been made to target year 7 students and a questionnaire to subject teachers invited them to identify students who were causing concern. Once social skills teaching is well established in a school it may be possible to run a rolling programme with different sets of skills being addressed in different groups each term. Individual students might attend one, two or three groups during the school year according to their needs. Staff at the school in question were aware that the groups for each term addressed a specific set of skills and that individual students would attend the group(s) most appropriate to their needs.

More detailed information may be collected about individual students and a pupil information form completed. An example of a student information form is included in Practice Pack (1), which can be found on the website.

The information about individual students will provide the information that is needed to select a group who share similar needs. Some staff have found it helpful to use a form which facilitates the translation of observed behaviour into social skills targets. A sample form is included in Practice Pack (2), which can be found on the website.

Once individual students have been selected on the basis of the target skills they might learn, the information can be summarized for all the group members and the target skills for the group sessions identified. Summary forms presented in Practice Packs (3)–(5) on the website.

At this point the students will not be aware that they are being considered for joining a social skills group and it is essential to engage them willingly in the whole process. Each student is usually interviewed and their perceptions of their social skills explored. A pupil questionnaire such as the one devised by Spence (1995) is often a useful way of eliciting student views and helping them to identify their own targets. The aims of the social skills group are discussed with the student and they are invited to sign their social skills contract. A sample contract is included in Practice Pack (6).

### 7.4.2 Involving parents

Social skills work is not yet a common feature of the secondary curriculum and so it will be necessary to explain the aims and objectives of such work either to all parents when their children join the school and/or to the parents of students who will be invited to join a social skills group. A sample letter to parents that might be used to inform them about a group is included in Practice Pack (7) together with a permission slip for them to return to the group leader. You may decide either to let the students deliver the letter to parents or to use the post.

It is often helpful to arrange to meet the parents so that they can ask questions about the group, particularly if it is intended to use video recording as a teaching device to give immediate feedback after role plays. A permission form authorizing the use of video recording is included in Practice Pack (8).

An open meeting also gives the opportunity to parents to discuss their role in generalizing the skills that are taught in the group by providing opportunities for their children to practice the skills at home as well as in the group and in the school community. If the group is to be evaluated, parents may be invited to complete a behavioural checklist in order to provide baseline data in the same way as subject teachers.

At the end of the group sessions, parents may welcome the opportunity to feedback to the group leaders any changes in their children's behaviour at home and/or repeat their checklist ratings.

### 7.4.3 Practical issues

Groups that invite identified participants and teach skills that are cumulative according to a planned programme are known as closed groups. The same students are involved in each session. This is in contrast to open groups such as Weight Watchers where different combinations of people may attend the sessions. The number of students in the group may vary according to the needs of the students and the aims of the group. For students who have SLCN rather than behavioural needs per se, a group size of six to eight would be appropriate. An even number is always useful for group activities and if there are over eight students in a group the waiting times for a turn in whole group activities can become tedious.

There are three key variables that should be considered when planning a group:

- *Gender mix.* It is often much easier to recruit boys than girls to a group because of the higher incidence (4:1 boys to girls) of SLCN in males. It is important to avoid having a singleton of either gender in a group unless you are confident about how that individual might respond.

- *Age range.* It is usual to restrict group membership to 1-year group. However, if the needs of the members are closely matched it is possible to widen the range (e.g. year 7 and 8, or even key stage) quite successfully.
- *The skills that the students need to learn.* As explained, when the selection of group members was discussed, students are selected for any one group according to the skills that they will learn in the group. It is important that other members of the staff team are aware of the selection criteria so that students who will not benefit from that particular group are not included.

The success of a group may depend on the balancing of the three variables to give a homogenous mix. One variable might be relaxed, provided that the other two are kept tight.

It is usual to have two group leaders or facilitators. Most people first learn to facilitate a group by acting as a co-leader with a more experienced colleague. Once the co-leader is confident, they can take the lead and work with a new co-leader so that the skills are cascaded among the staff team. In schools the leaders/co-leaders might be a speech and language therapist, an educational psychologist, teacher, inclusion worker or a teaching assistant, or any other professional who has the relevant skills. Two adults are needed for many reasons:

- One acts as an activity leader while the other observes the responses of the individual students. In some groups the adults may take turns to lead the activity and to observe.
- The two adults can model role plays for the students to observe and comment.
- If equipment such as video or audio recording is involved, one person may manage the group while the other acts as technician.
- At the end of each session there is time planned to discuss and reflect on the activities, the process and the response of each student. The two adults collaborate to write session notes and finalize the planning for the next session.
- It is time consuming to liaise with both staff and parents about the target skills for the week and the generalization activities. This task may effectively be shared between the two adults.

Many secondary schools do have a suitable room which can be timetabled for the group sessions and 'booked out' for the duration of the group, usually eight to ten sessions. An ideal venue would be:

- a group room rather than a classroom with space to rearrange the furniture and move around freely

- timetabled to be available on a regular basis
- free from interruptions
- away from obvious distractions.

Timetabling the sessions may be difficult unless the senior management and the whole staff team support the introduction of social skills training. Some options that have been shown to work include:

- Early sessions which start before the teaching day. This involved students arriving early (with the support of parents) and missing registration.
- Students withdrawn from PHSE sessions which were timetabled at the same time for the whole year group.
- An after school or lunchtime club. The latter has become less practical as school reduces the lunch break.
- Using learning support time if students are already timetabled for this.
- Any regular time, even if it involves missing a particular subject. Trying to vary the time so that students do not miss the same lesson is usually the least successful option.

### 7.4.4 Planning for a group

The group leaders take the lead in planning the group and it is important that they are allocated time to do this. At the school that ran a rolling programme of groups, a half term was allowed to plan each group. The planning cycle for the year 7/8 groups in one school is represented in Figure 7.3.

The first task of the teachers/facilitators is to gather baseline assessment information and analyze the needs of the students. Students are allocated to the groups on the basis of their needs but with regard to the balance of the group for year, gender, and whether the students have issues that would make it hard for them to learn together. Once the needs of the students have been identified it should be possible to plan the focus for

| Autumn term | | Spring term | | Summer term | |
|---|---|---|---|---|---|
| Run 2nd phase of transition group | Run Group 1 | Run Group 2 | Run Group 3 | Run Group 4 | Run group 5 transition group |
| Plan Group 1 | Plan Group 2 | Plan Group 3 | Plan Group 4 | Plan Group 5 (transition group) | |

**Figure 7.3** The planning cycle.

each session and decide how many sessions will be needed in order to address the targets that have been identified.

The sessions are planned to follow a standard structure. The warm-up and closing activities for each session remain the same each week. This helps the students to make the transitions from class to group and then back to class. A clear transition is important because the social rules and behaviours within the group will be different from those that are expected in a subject lesson. A standard session structure that has been used successfully over many years is shown below:

- welcome and warm up activity
- review ground rules, if necessary
- review of generalization exercise from the previous week
- introduction of the new topic
- three activities to practice the target skill
- set generalization exercise for the following week
- closing activity and relaxation.

An individual session plan (see website) follows the standard structure as illustrated for a session with the focus of 'asking and responding to questions'.

The activities mentioned in the session plan are discussed in the Practice Pack – Activities and Games for Social Skills Groups.

At the end of each session the two leaders/facilitators should spend time evaluating the session. The time to do this debriefing is when the session is fresh in the mind. An agenda for debriefing might be:

- content of the session – choices of activity – pace of the session
- enjoyment levels
- participation, interaction of group members
- environmental factors (e.g. distractions, lighting)
- individual pupil session evaluations

A series of proformas are included in the Practice Pack, available on the website:

- a checklist for setting up a social skills group
- session planning form
- session evaluation form
- a form for informing parents/teachers about the 'homework' for the week; this week's 'targets' – so that they are able to support generalization of the target skills
- a record of generalization targets.

### 7.4.5 Techniques for social skills groups

There is a range of techniques that are used regularly in running social skills groups. The techniques are selected flexibly to demonstrate and practice the target skills for each session.

#### 7.4.5.1 Modelling

The role of modelling in the learning of behaviour was first introduced by Bandura (1969) when he described how children learn by watching the behaviour of others. In a social skills group, adults set up a situation to model appropriate or inappropriate behaviour. A typical example might involve listening skills:

- The adults model a conversation with one of them demonstrating poor listening skills by showing a range of code violations.
- Students observe/record the code violations.
- The code violations are discussed by the group.
- The adults or students then model the appropriate behaviours, repairing the original model.
- Students work in threes and take turns to be speaker, listener and observer. The observer has a checklist to record the signs of good listening shown by the listener. **Students in any modelling exercise only practice the target skills – the positive behaviours**. We never ask them to show the code violations which might inadvertently be reinforced.
- Students feedback the positive experiences to the whole group.

#### 7.4.5.2 Role rehearsal: the practice of new skills

 Once the new skills have been identified and demonstrated, activities can be selected to practice and reinforce the skills. A sample session for asking and responding to questions is available on the website.

#### 7.4.5.3 Role play

Role play may use scenarios that are provided by the facilitators to illustrate a particular skill such as joining a conversation. Alternatively, and sometimes more powerfully, the facilitators may use real-life scenarios that the students have experienced (e.g. an incident of teasing). The group may then co-operate to write a script or scripts which describe an adaptive response to the situation. Students then take roles in the script and each has a turn to practice the target skill and take on the other roles in the scenario. This 'walk the walk' technique in role play helps students to understand the perspective of all the participants in an incident.

For individual students who find a particular situation hard, it may be helpful to adapt the social script that the group has written into the form of a personal social story or a comic strip conversation (Gray, 1994).

### 7.4.5.4 Sculpting

Sculpting is a non-verbal technique that is particularly useful when working with students who find it hard to express themselves using spoken language. Events, feelings and problems can be represented visually. For example, adolescents might be asked to represent their feelings about certain lessons by placing themselves in relation to a chair which represented the lesson. The placings can be mapped on a diagram and the significance of the placements discussed in the group. Students can be encouraged to use non-verbal communication as a freeze-frame to enhance the representation and to practice non-verbal communication skills.

### 7.4.5.5 Generalization

Students may become confident about using new social skills in the controlled, structured environment of the group but singularly fail to use those skills in their daily lives. Structured generalization activities are, therefore, planned into each group session. Students are asked to choose the 'when', 'where' and 'who' they will target for practice outside the group. A record form for 'generalization targets' is provided in the Practice Pack for students to record their practice of the skills between sessions. At the start of each session the facilitators will ask the students for feedback on their generalization targets.

### 7.4.6 Pragmatic skills: interventions for students

Students who have specific problems with the skills that are needed for a successful conversational exchange may be selected to work together to practice the skills. Good role models are provided by the adult facilitators so there is no requirement to include students for whom the skills are so automatic and fluent that they would find it hard to identify what they do in order to maintain an interaction. The areas that students find particularly hard are listed below:

- how and when to initiate a conversation
- turn taking in conversation, topic maintenance
- good listening
- ending a conversation
- reading and providing non-verbal cues, facial expression/tone of voice/proxemics/body language
- adjusting a conversation to the needs of different people.

The pragmatic checklist for teachers is in Practice Pack (13) on the website.

These areas may be the focus for a group session or sessions. Clearly the non-verbal aspects of communication will need to be addressed over a number of sessions. Whenever possible the skills that have been the focus of previous sessions are revised and monitored during subsequent sessions.

Detailed session plans are on the website for:

- how and when to initiate a conversation
- taking turns in a conversation
- taking the role of speaker and listener
- ending a conversation
- reading and signalling non-verbal cues
- adapting what is said to the needs of the audience
- giving an appropriate amount of detail.

Each of the sample session plans was introduced using the same warm-up activities and closing activities.

### 7.4.6.1 Warm-up activities

The same warm-up activities and closing activities can be used for each group session:

- Welcome to the group.
- Something good
  - Facilitator says: 'I am ...... and since we met I (went for a walk and saw some deer) ...'.
  - Facilitator calls the name of a group member. Eye contact is established. Facilitator throws the bean bag/soft toy to the group member.
  - Group member says: 'I am ...... and since we met I...'.
  - The activity continues until everyone has had a turn.
- Empty chair
  - An empty chair is introduced into the circle.
  - Facilitator/students says: 'I have an empty chair on my right/left and I would like ...... to sit by me.' Remember to decide which before starting the activity and practice to be sure that everyone knows their right/left.
  - The named student makes eye contact and moves to sit in the empty chair.
  - The activity continues until everyone has had a turn with the facilitator intervening sensitively if someone is left out.
- Review the target activities from the previous session.
- The focus of the session is introduced to the group.

### 7.4.6.2 Closing activity

- Strength cards
  - Each group member is asked in turn to pick a strength card for the person on their right/left. The 'strength' is a quality that the person has

shown during the session (e.g. listening well). Students are encouraged
to say why they picked that card.

  ○ The recipient takes the card, makes eye contact and says: 'Thank you'.
• Relaxation exercise.
• Goodbye and good luck with the weekly target(s).

Some well-tried and tested activities to use in social skills groups are
presented on the website Activities for Social Skills Groups.

The focus for the sessions that have been presented is on social interaction
and successful communication. The skills that are selected are practiced
over as many sessions as is necessary for the group members. In some cases
it may take months, or even years, to acquire the skills to a level of fluency.
Some students may benefit from more one-on-one support from an adult
between the group sessions to develop the skills but it is important that
they continue to practice the skills in the group of peers.

### 7.4.7 Activities for social skill development

In the section about planning a social skills group an emphasis was placed
on the analysis of the needs of the student and how to plan group sessions
around those needs. It is very tempting to decide to run a social skills
group and pick up an off-the-shelf programme to follow. However good
these generic programmes may be, they are not designed around the needs
of a specific group of students and many people are disappointed by their
outcome measures because the sessions have not been tightly targeted to
the needs of the members of the group. It is important to identify the
needs of the students and plan the focus for the sessions before consulting
the books of games and activities. The activities may then be selected so
that they reinforce the theme of the session that has been planned.

---

**Points to remember**

• Pragmatic difficulties may be secondary features associated with
  SLCN and do not, therefore, equate to an autistic spectrum disorder.
• The pragmatic aspects of language can be analyzed and taught to
  students in social skills groups.
• Pragmatics involve both the verbal and non-verbal aspects of
  communication.
• Social skills training is effective when it is targeted at the skills the stu-
  dents need to learn and the skills are generalized into real-life settings.

# 8

# Talking Behaviour

**Chapter Objectives**

> To establish the link between unidentified SLCN and challenging behaviour at secondary school

> To help teachers to understand some of the common behavioural responses of these students

> To raise awareness that 70–90% of students who are excluded from school and are educated in pupil referral units have unacknowledged SLCN

> To establish the importance of the recognition of SLCN at secondary school and how the interventions set out in earlier chapters may be used to support students at risk of exclusion

## 8.1 Introduction

Studies of young children have shown that the warning signs of difficulties with social interaction associated with language impairment may be apparent even in pre-school settings. Hadley and Rice (1991) found that 'Pre-schoolers behave as if they know who talks well and who does not and they prefer to interact with those who do.' Children whose speech was difficult to understand and whose grammar was poor had fewer social interactions than other children. They, therefore, had fewer opportunities to practice their language skills and to enjoy successful encounters with others.

The children who are most likely to be identified as having SLI are those who experience phonological problems which affect the intelligibility of their speech and who then go on to struggle with the acquisition of literacy skills (Bishop and Adams, 1992). Children who have less obvious problems with receptive or expressive language may not be recognized as having language problems (Beitchman, 1985) but are often referred to support services for other reasons such as slow educational progress, poor reading comprehension or challenging behaviour. A surprising number of these children may not be identified as having SLI until they are in the secondary phase of their education (Ripley *et al.*, 2001). Andy did make the transition to secondary school but did not survive the social, linguistic and academic challenge for long before he was permanently excluded. Harry appears to be following a similar trajectory. For some students like Harvey, interventions can be effective, even when the area of difficulty is only recognized in year 9.

 Case study: Harry

Harry transferred to secondary school with a history of behaviour problems at primary school and a BESD Statement of Special Educational Needs. He had worked with the Behaviour Support Team and had been on a part-time timetable in year 5 but had been reintegrated into a full timetable for year 6. There had been four fixed-term exclusions in year 6.

A few weeks into year 7 Harry started to refuse to attend many of his lessons despite having one-on-one LSA support. He stayed on the site of the campus but would stay outside even in inclement weather.

Assessments at primary school had indicated that he had above average non-verbal skills but he had been reluctant to engage with any language-based tasks. His file shows that Harry had speech problems when of pre-school age and these phonological problems affected his acquisition of literacy skills, which remained low. Reports from his subject teachers suggested that Harry had more general SLI which would merit investigation:

- He did not follow instructions but responded to visual support.
- His vocabulary knowledge was described as 'patchy'.
- He found it hard to work with his peers and interact socially with them.
- He was able to participate in subjects which are less verbally loaded such as PE and art and usually attended these classes.

While there are clearly many factors contributing to Harry's present difficulties, there is prima facie evidence that SLI may have contributed. Several appointments have been made to assess Harry's language profile in more detail, but for now he will not come into school to meet the EP or speech and language therapist.

 Case study: Harvey

Harvey was referred to the EPS in the summer term of year 9 for disruptive behaviour. He had received literacy support at primary school and his parents had sought a diagnosis of both dyslexia and attention deficit disorder.

At the start of year 10 assessment indicated that Harvey had language skills at first centile and that he was finding it hard to access the abstract, context-free language (CALP) which is the main medium for teaching and learning in key stage 3/4. In addition, he had more specific problems with word finding and categorization. Strategies were put in place to address his core language problems and behaviour was no longer the focus of the interventions.

If teachers are not aware that a student in their class has SLI, the behavioural responses of the student may give rise to misperceptions of primary problems such as:

- emotional and behavioural problems (Gordon, 1991)
- stubbornness and non-compliance (Freeman and Willig, 1995)
- low motivation and disinterest (Moats and Lyon, 1993).

## 8.2 The 'Seven Deadly Sins'

Consultations with staff about students who are subsequently found to have SLI have frequently led to descriptions of behaviour which can be identified as the 'Seven Deadly Sins'.

### 8.2.1 Uncooperative and challenging

Andy was described as confrontational and abusive to staff. From the language perspective, a failure to respond to requests and instructions because of limited understanding may be interpreted as defiance, as in the case of Barry. By key stage 3 a pattern of not expecting to understand will have become well entrenched and for students like Andy this will, only too frequently, lead to inappropriate behavioural responses in the classroom. Long-standing difficulties with understanding the rules of the classroom or the playground may have social implications for relationships with both adults and peers. Andy was described as volatile and aggressive towards other students.

### 8.2.2 Surly

Like Brenda, Hugh was perceived as not responsive to adults.

Case study: Hugh, Year 9

Despite an earlier history of comprehension difficulties, problems with word-retrieval and severe literacy difficulties, Hugh entered secondary school with a statement of special educational needs, which described his needs as being primarily concerned with behaviour. Speech and language therapy assessment found that many of Hugh's rather curt and defensive responses to questions stemmed from his anticipation that he would be misunderstood and would say something wrong or, to him, 'stupid'. His teachers adopted a less questioning approach and built on his initial responses by signalling he was on the right track. This produced a significant change in his behaviour.

### 8.2.3 Unmotivated

Andy refused to engage with tasks in the classroom and never attempted homework, whereas Harry frequently refused even to enter a classroom if he anticipated that he would not understand a lesson. Years of facing learning challenges without experiencing much success had clearly influenced the behaviour of both these students. Students with a history of SLI may also have consistently failed to remember what they have been told in instructions, only remember part of an instruction and get it wrong, or fail to bring vital materials or homework to lessons with the inevitable consequences.

### 8.2.4 Odd or strange

 Case study: Hector

Hector had a statement of SEN from primary school when he transferred to secondary school and had been excluded in year 6. He had a history of delayed and disordered language development which had affected his acquisition of literacy skills. At secondary school he refused to attempt reading or writing tasks without LSA support. When he perceived tasks as difficult, Hector would tear up his work, hide under the table, make loud animal noises or storm out of the room.

Hector appeared quite odd to his year 7 peers when he hid under tables in some lessons. Students with SLI may seem odd for a range of reasons to do with their processing of language whether or not they also have the pragmatic difficulties that are discussed in Chapter 6.

- Students with difficulties processing spoken language may respond to only part of an instruction or to a key word in an utterance. This may result in what are known as off-target responses which sound unusual to the listener; for example,

  Q: 'Why did Hitler invade Poland?'

  A: 'Plumbers' (in 2006 there was a popular belief that there had been a gold rush of Polish plumbers to the UK).

- Literal interpretations of figurative speech. Some subjects attract the use of non-literal language (e.g. English) and some teachers are more likely than others to use non-literal language in their explanations or instructions (Marshman, 1998); for example,

  Student waits his turn for the long jump pit.

  PE Teacher: 'Off you go then'.

  Student turns and walks away.

- Students who do not reliably recall the phonological code for key words may make substitutions which sound amusing to others in the class; for example,

  Q: What do we call it when birds fly south for the winter?

  A: Vibrate (peers snigger)

In contrast, a student may wonder why the birds have a bad headache (migraine) and miss the next few exchanges while they try to make some sense of their interpretation.

## 8.2.5 Liar

A positive strategy if you do not understand a question is often to say 'yes' and smile. Students may have learned that this usually pleases an adult and that there is a better than 50% chance that this was the required response.

Another strategy, if you find it hard to organize your expressive language, is to agree with or repeat what another student has already said – even if it is quite obvious to an observer that your experiment did not have the same outcome.

If your speech is hard to understand and/or you have expressive problems it may be easier to deny any involvement in events that you are questioned about and, if pressed to respond, to use 'abusive language' like Andy. Some students may decide always to say 'yes' when asked if they understand, have finished, have done what they have been instructed to do because it is too difficult to attempt to explain 'why' if the real answer is 'no'.

## 8.2.6 Aggressive

As children develop they learn to use language to influence and control the behaviour of other people (Baker and Cantwell, 1987). If language development does not progress in the usual way, children are likely to continue to attempt to control their environment by physical means: the grabbing of toys by toddlers is tolerated but we teach them to ask for a turn as a more acceptable response. Students who are not able to use language for a range of functions and purposes are more likely to continue to attempt to control their social environment by physical means rather than by verbal negotiation.

The evidence suggests that students referred to psychiatric services who have undetected SLI have a higher incidence of 'neurotic' behaviour (Cohen, 1998).

Parents also rate their sons with SLI as having a higher incidence of aggressive/hyperactive behaviour (Aram *et al.*, 1984).

## 8.2.7 Stupid

Readers who have had the misfortune to know friends or relatives who have suffered a stroke will be acutely aware of how people respond differently to those who have unusual or unintelligible speech, even if they have known them prior to the onset of their disability. Hadley and Rice (1991) identified how children at pre-school respond differently to peers who had speech and expressive language problems. This pattern of more limited, positive, social interactions may persist over time. Neutral adults may not take the time to listen to people who are unable to express themselves clearly and dismiss them as 'thick' or 'retards'. The young person may respond by withdrawing from social encounters as much as possible or by using physical means to express their frustrations.

## 8.3 The links between language impairment and behaviour problems: the evidence

The behaviour problems of young children who have been identified as having SLI have been well documented since the early 1980s (Beadle, 1979).

Botting and Conti-Ramsden (2000) identified 40% of the children in their samples as having anti-social or emotional problems, in addition to their SLI. The majority of the studies that have established that children with SLI are at risk of developing behavioural problems have tracked the children during their early years and found that as language skills improved, the behaviour difficulties ameliorated (Stevenson *et al.*, 1985). By definition these were children whose language impairment was recognized and who had received appropriate intervention. However, some of these individuals will transfer to secondary school with their language needs still unresolved. If the needs are assessed, it is possible to provide effective support as set out in the preceding chapters, even if this takes some time to put in place as with Harvey.

There are students who enter year 7 with language problems which have not been identified and who are perceived as having a primary behavioural, emotional, social difficulties (BESD). Some of these students may be permanently excluded from mainstream school, like Andy, Harold and Harry, and find themselves in special provision for students with BESD. In the past decade there has been increasing awareness of the links between SLI and BESD because of studies of the language profiles of students in specialist provision.

### 8.3.1 Research evidence

- Camarata et al. (1988) found that in students with mild-to-moderate BESD 71% had significant language problems.
- Burgess and Bransby (1990) found that of 17 students in a BESD unit aged 6–12 years, 16 of them had SLI sufficient to require speech and language therapy and 11 had 'severe' SLI. The students had been perceived as deviant and uncooperative. Their speech was intelligible so problems with receptive and expressive language had not been identified. As for many students with BESD, management of therapy at the unit was language based.
- Warr-Leeper (1994) looked at boys in a residential treatment centre – 80% had undetected language problems.
- Heneker (2005) noted that of 11 students in a pupil referral unit (PRU) aged 5–11 years 91% had some difficulties with communication.

The four research studies quoted had examined the language profiles of students who were already in special provision. Ripley and Yuill (2005) investigated the cognitive profiles of boys who had been excluded from school in a shire county during the academic year 1999–2000 and compared them with the profiles of a matched group of control students. The average age of the students in the two groups was 13 years 2 months. The results from the study showed the following:

- The non-verbal abilities of the excluded pupils and the control group were not significantly different.

- The verbal skills of the excluded pupils were significantly impaired when compared with the control group.
- Two-thirds of the excluded students had speech and language impairments.
- Expressive language problems were more closely linked to behaviour problems for children over 8 years of age.
- Excluded students with expressive language impairment had a high incidence of co-morbid emotional problems.
- Excluded students with SLI had a long history of difficult relationships with their peers.

The evidence for a strong association between behaviour problems and exclusions from school continues to stack up. However, at the point of exclusion we are often surprisingly unaware that the students have a 70–90% estimated risk of language impairment that plays a significant role in driving the inappropriate behaviour.

## 8.3.2 Breaking the cycle

The evidence suggests that children who have language problems at 3 years of age are at risk of developing behaviour problems by the age of 8 years (Stevenson *et al.*, 1985). However, the positive news is that if the language needs of the children are identified and they respond to interventions, the behaviour problems decrease as the children's language skills improve (Stevenson *et al.*, 1985). Unfortunately, if children progress through the education system without their language needs being identified and appropriate support put in place, the behavioural difficulties may escalate to the point of exclusion from primary school like Harold or during key stage 3 like Andy and Harry. Encounters with students such as Andy and Harry have shown that by key stage 3 they are difficult to assess because they actively avoid any situations in which they might feel challenged. In the Heneker study of students in a PRU (2005), the students who were allocated SLT made good progress with their language targets and gained confidence as communicators but the behavioural outcomes were reported as 'variable'. However, just one term of appropriate intervention by the SLT and the modification of the learning environment in the classroom were unlikely to be sufficient to break the cycle of patterns of behaviour built up over many years. Although this study focused on SLT intervention, other studies including the experience of working with Hugh and Harvey suggest that modifications to the learning environment and the expectations of key adults can be effective in bringing about changes in behaviour patterns that have been built up over many years (Figure 8.1).

The strategies for working with students who have SLCN which are set out in the Chapters 2–7 have all stood the test of time and proved effective for most, if not all, students. The strategies are essentially school-based

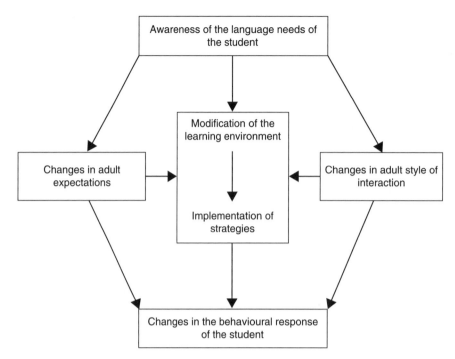

**Figure 8.1** Changes due to key adults.

interventions rather than therapeutic procedures, which are carried out exclusively by speech and language therapists. Everyone learns language most effectively when they are experiencing and using the language in the context of their social lives, the curriculum or their work place. A framework of intervention is presented in Figure 8.2.

For some students who have expressive language problems, one of their key problems is the ability to give an account of themselves when their behaviour is challenged. They may struggle to explain the events that led up to a confrontation with another student and may, by default, take more blame than may be appropriate. They are not as skilled as their peers at negotiating their way out of trouble when found in the wrong place at the wrong time, when homework is late, or when something gets lost or broken. The difficulty in these instances is linked to their limited ability to create a personal narrative, as discussed in Chapter 6, 'Talking Language'. The framework of the narrative approach can be used to support the students to structure their coping strategies for events that they consistently fail to resolve appropriately.

In order to break the cycle it is important first to look beyond the presenting behaviours and investigate what may be precipitating the challenging behaviour. As Baker and Cantwell (1987) assert:

> A child with SLI is frequently under pressure to conform (or perform) in situations where their ability to respond is compromised. The result may be tantrums, behaviour problems, attention and arousal problems but all too often the behaviour becomes the focus of 'treatment'.

The evidence suggests that over 70% of students with behaviour problems are likely to experience underlying SLCN. Chapter 9 discusses some ways in which teaching staff might begin to investigate whether a student may have SLCN and gather evidence that may then be used as the basis of a referral to support agencies. In many areas an SLT service is not routinely available in key stage 3/4 and so a referral to the EPS may be the first option to be considered. Once the SLCN of the student have been identi-fied an intervention can be planned which will include modifications to the learning environment and the implementation of strategies to meet the specific needs of the student following some of the ideas set out in Chapters 2–7 of this book. Some small group work with a focus on social skills may be required for the majority of the students because, as Hadley and Rice (1991) found, children who have SLI begin to have less rich and successful social interactions than their peers from their pre-school days.

If a referral is made to the Child and Mental Health Service it will be important for that team to be aware that the student has SLCN so that their therapeutic approach is not based on a language-loaded model.

The evidence shows that the early recognition of language difficulties and early intervention will ameliorate the emotional and social consequences

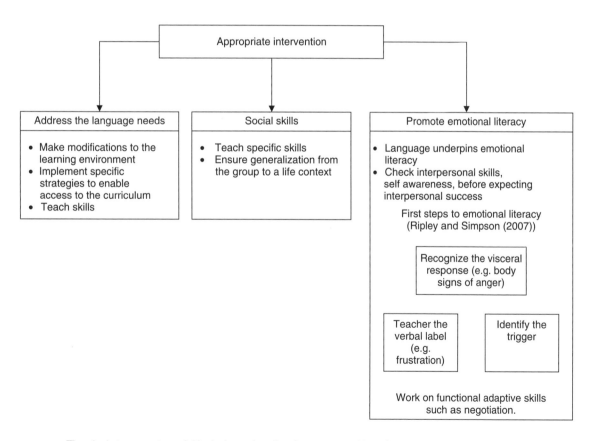

The aim is to promote social inclusion, educational progress and to reduce exclusions from school.

**Figure 8.2** Framework of intervention.

of a language impairment. However, many of the students who transfer to secondary school with their language needs not identified will show a range of challenging behaviours. The task is to recognize the language needs of the student and plan appropriate interventions.

> **Points to remember**
>
> - Students may enter secondary school without their SLCN having been recognized.
> - Students who have unrecognized SLCN are significantly at risk of behavioural difficulties and exclusion from school.
> - Intervention, even at secondary school, by providing modifications to the learning environment and changing adult expectations can be effective in changing behavioural responses that have been established over time.

# Assessing Speech and Language

> **Chapter Objectives**
>
> > **To support teachers in their frontline role of identifying students who have SLCN**
> > **To describe the contributions that other professionals might make to a multi-disciplinary assessment**
> > **To describe the unique role that teachers and LSAs have in the multi-disciplinary assessment of students through structured observations, standardized assessment procedures and language sampling**

## 9.1 Introduction to assessment

SLI (speech and language impairment) is one of a family of complex neuro-developmental disorders that may be identified in childhood. There is evidence (Rutter, 2007) that SLI is separate from other neurological disorders but it may show considerable overlap with other neuro-developmental disorders at a behavioural level. Many developmental disorders do show overlapping endophenotypes and it is all too easy to be misled into making short-cut assumptions about the significance of certain behaviours, such as the avoidance of eye contact, and label students inappropriately. Reflect for a moment about all the reasons a person may avoid eye contact – perhaps when a teacher or a lecturer asks for volunteers? Also, without an understanding of a student's needs, behaviour may be misinterpreted. For example, Hugh in Chapter 8 was perceived as curt and defensive in his response to adults. A comprehensive assessment is, therefore, important so that we can understand the needs of a student in order to support them in an appropriate way. Many students who enter secondary school will have had their needs identified and the appropriate records will have been sent on from the primary school. However, others, as discussed in Chapter 8, may have their underlying language needs masked by secondary difficulties, particularly with literacy or behaviour. Teachers may be the first professionals at any point in the education system to become aware of a student's SLCN because they observe that:

- Communication with adults and peers is problematic and having consequences for their social, emotional development and behaviour.
- Language difficulties are disrupting learning and access to the curriculum, putting them at risk for educational under-achievement.

The opportunity to observe students over time and to reflect on how they respond in different settings and to different educational challenges may give teachers a valuable insight into the nature and impact of the SLCN of a student. It is important, therefore, that teachers are fully included in a multi-disciplinary approach to the assessment of SLCN. This same principle applies to other neuro-developmental disorders such as ASC or ADHD if we are to ensure that a reliable profile of an individual's needs is established.

The good practice guidelines for the assessment of any complex neuro-developmental disorder recommend that assessment should:

- Be multi-agency, involving a range of professionals who will bring different perspectives to the assessment.
- Involve assessment over time. The parents are usually a valuable source of information about a student's developmental history and all assessments will include a family history element. One of the advantages for parents of the common assessment framework (CAF) should be that they will only need to tell their 'story' once, rather than successively to different professionals. However, school records will also hold valuable information about the student over time: how they have responded to educational and social challenges and how they have responded to different support strategies.
- Involve assessment over a range of settings. A student would be expected to behave differently at home, at an assessment clinic, in the classroom, on the playground or during an individual interview with familiar or an unfamiliar adult. It is only by combining all these perspectives that a reliable picture of a student's communication skills may be compiled.

The core multi-agency team members who would be able to bring a unique perspective to an assessment of SLCN include:

- parents
- teachers
- classroom assistants
- speech and language therapists
- educational psychologists
- paediatricians.

Some students may benefit from additional assessment by therapists such as the paediatric occupational therapist or by child and adolescent psychiatrists.

The outcome of a multi-disciplinary assessment should, ideally, be a consensus view of the needs of the student and the formulation of a comprehensive plan of how the student may be supported socially, emotionally, linguistically and academically.

## 9.2  Standardized procedures

Many standardized tests of language are designed to ascertain the student's attainment relative to that of young people of the same age. Unfortunately, many of the standardized procedures are designed for use with children of primary school age and are 'closed' tests (i.e. are intended to be administered by speech and language therapists or psychologists). There are some language assessments that are available for use by trained teachers (e.g. British Picture Vocabulary Scale (BPVS)) (Dunn *et al.*, 1997) or Peter and the Cat, Narrative Assessment (Leitão and Allan (2003)) but the picture materials are targeted at children of primary school age. Reading comprehension is a key indicator of receptive language difficulties when the decoding (reading accuracy) is more competent. Reading assessments are routinely carried out in schools. However, most standardized procedures usually require the involvement of outside agencies such as a speech and language therapist or educational psychologist.

## 9.3  Language profiling

This is usually carried out by the analysis of language using a language sample. Teaching staff and teaching assistants may be asked to record language samples for the assessment of expressive language by a speech and language therapist or psychologist. Oral language is the usual source of a language sample, but sometimes it is possible to analyze a written language sample.

## 9.4  Teacher-based assessment

### 9.4.1  Assessment in the context of the classroom

Teachers and classroom assistants are often best placed to carry out assessment over time in the context of the classroom: the ecological approach.

Subject teachers at secondary school may not meet individual students frequently but they will have the opportunity to observe their response to their subject and the learning environment provided by their teaching style. The classroom assistant may have a different contribution to make to an assessment because they may be able to observe how the same student responds in different settings through the day.

By the time students reach secondary school it is generally assumed that they will be able to meet the goals for effective speaking and listening as defined by the DfES (1995):

- To listen, understand and respond appropriately to others (a mixed receptive language and pragmatic goal).
- To use the vocabulary and grammar of spoken, standard English (an expressive language goal).
- To formulate, clarify and express their ideas (language as a medium for thought and an expressive language goal).
- To adapt their speech (meaning expressive language rather than speech production) to a widening range of circumstances and demands. Students who have communication problems may find it particularly hard to make alterations in the way that they address different people and to understand subtle variations in language use.

 Class-based staff will be able to observe these aspects of communication with both adults and peers and can collect evidence in a systematic way. A framework for structured observations and a short observation checklist may be found on the website.

### 9.4.2 Individual assessment of a student

Subject teachers and TAs may become aware of the receptive and/or expressive language problems of a student and discuss their concerns with the SENCO. The SENCO may decide to carry out some further assessments of the student and refer back to any standard assessments that have already been carried out such as the CAT tests that many schools administer at the start of year 7, or the results of any reading and spelling assessments carried out either at secondary or primary school.

In Chapter 5, 'Clear About Speech', the link between phonological processing and learning the skills of decoding for reading and encoding for spelling was discussed. Eighty percent of students who have problems with reading and spelling at secondary school will have a history of SLI. However, there are some students who may appear to read adequately according to their reading scores but have difficulties with understanding a text. These students, the poor comprehenders, are at risk for also having difficulties with understanding the spoken language of the classroom and, possibly, the fast-moving verbal exchanges of their peers. An individual assessment of reading accuracy and reading comprehension is, therefore, a good starting point for investigating the language difficulties of the student.

Literacy support in the classroom would follow the same strategies as for dyslexic students but additional support to access the spoken language of the classroom is indicated for the poor comprehenders.

Some SENCOs have access to standardized language assessments which are open tests. The British Picture Vocabulary Scale (BPVS) is an open test and would provide an assessment of receptive vocabulary levels. More informal approaches to language assessment can provide qualitative information. This might involve activities such as defining words (a meta-linguistic  task), providing synonyms (e.g. 'Can you think of another word for an "author"?'), or thinking of alternative meanings for the same word (e.g. 'bat'). These are tasks that students with language problems are likely to find more difficult than their peers. A detailed assessment of a language profile may be carried out using the checklist on the website.

Studies of students in key stage 1 who have intelligible speech but experience hidden language problems have identified four key areas of difficulty which are the 'markers' for language problems. These may be easily adapted to the secondary context.

### 9.4.2.1 Immaturities of expressive grammar

It is possible to carry out grammatical analysis by examining the written language of a student or by listening to samples of their expressive language. Immaturities may be identified in the areas of use of verb tenses, use of a range of vocabulary, use of connectives, use of subordinate clauses and the sentence structure that is used. Sometimes it is possible to identify some residual phonological problems when the student attempts to use or is asked to repeat polysyllabic words, particularly the unfamiliar polysyllabic words which may be part of new topic vocabulary.

### 9.4.2.2 Narrative skills

Students who have SLCN often find it hard to sequence the main ideas to construct a personal narrative. It is possible to assess this skill by asking students to:

- give an account of an activity they have just completed (e.g. a science experiment)
- repeat a familiar story or give a résumé of an episode of a favourite TV programme
- re-tell a novel story that has just been read to them.

Narrative skill is important educationally (producing a written narrative), and socially (the ability to explain emotionally charged events to avoid trouble).

### 9.4.2.3 Numerical ability

The early number curriculum is heavily loaded with abstract conceptual ideas which may seem simple to an adult (e.g. the ideas of time, place, measurement and contrasts, e.g. short/tall, add/subtract). Some students may have overcome these early conceptual problems and have made adequate progress with maths. However, they may be stronger in the visual-spatial aspects of maths (e.g. geometry) than the more abstract aspects such as algebra. New mathematical concepts may be particularly difficult to acquire.

### 9.4.2.4 Reading comprehension

Reading comprehension is a strong marker of language comprehension at all ages. Students who have limited reading skills may be slower to develop vocabulary than their peers because from mid-childhood new vocabulary is acquired through reading as well as via spoken language.

The observations that are carried out in the classroom, together with any additional evidence from teacher-based assessment, will provide a valuable contribution to the multi-disciplinary assessment of the language needs of a student. Without this frontline evidence, which leads to a request for the involvement of other professionals, the language needs of students may all too easily be overlooked.

## 9.5 Assessment by the educational psychologist

Once a student is in school, the educational psychologist may be the first 'outside agency' to be contacted when there are concerns about either learning or behaviour. Many of the case studies illustrated how SLCN may not be the perceived need at the time of the initial referral. However, clues in the way in which the student is described by teachers on the referral form, during consultation meetings or in response to a behavioural questionnaire will often provide the first step in the analysis of the student's needs.

The role of the EP as a member of a multi-disciplinary assessment team might be summarized as:

- to clarify the nature of the speech, language, communication needs, in collaboration with colleagues

- to access the implications for learning
- to assess the classroom as a learning environment for the student
- to assess the implications for access to the National Curriculum
- to identify the social, emotional and behavioural implications of the student's SLCN.

In order to meet these aims, the EP will use a range of strategies.

Once the educational psychologist has an understanding of the language profile of the student and how this affects their learning, social interaction and emotional/behavioural response, it should be possible to advise about a range of issues which might include:

- Modifications to the delivery of the curriculum such as the provision of visual support for learning and the differentiation of teacher language in the classroom.
- Strategies to address the associated problems with literacy skills which affect access to the curriculum. At the age of 16 years, 49% of students who have a history of SLCN would be expected to experience problems with the accuracy of reading (decoding). However, 74% will experience difficulties with the comprehension of a text and this may be less immediately obvious than the difficulties associated with decoding (Conti-Ramsden and Botting, 1999).
- The development of social skills and social communication skills, as described in Chapter 7.
- Advice on the management of the behavioural difficulties which have become associated with the SLCN.

## 9.6 A medical perspective: the role of the paediatrician

The role of the paediatrician is to identify any medical, genetic or treatable conditions such as hearing loss, which are co-morbid with SLI (Baird, 2007). Most students with SLCN will have had paediatric involvement long before they reach secondary school. Some conditions are easily identified in the early years, such as the oro-motor problems that affect feeding, eating and speech development or structural problems such as a cleft palate. It is estimated that about 4% of speech problems have an underlying medical cause. A hearing loss may be acquired through illness or trauma and must not, therefore, be discounted when considering the language problems of older students.

Students who have SLI which is associated with general learning difficulties are more likely to have some underlying genetic or medical aetiology for their language disorder or delay (e.g. Down's syndrome or fragile X).

Family histories of students who present with SLCN indicate that in 50% of cases a family member will also have experienced some degree of SLCN. The evidence suggests that clusters of genes on chromosomes 16 and 19 are implicated in SLI, but genetic investigations and genetic counselling are not routinely carried out for the majority of children who have SLCN.

## 9.7 Assessment by the speech and language therapist

The majority of students receiving speech and language therapy at secondary school will already be on the 'books' of the local therapy service. However, some may have recently moved into the area or fallen through the net because their current needs have not been recognized.

The main purposes of assessment by the speech and language therapist are:

- to ascertain whether a problem exists
- if it does, what sort of problem is it?
- do students meet the criteria for intervention?
- to indicate the possible goals of intervention
- to measure change in the problem, over time, with or without intervention.

Assessment will include:

1 Information gathering using proformas, checklists and a case history.
2 The initial assessment. This uses both formal and informal procedures to assess 'competence' which refers to their core skills. Students are also observed in class, to assess how they understand and use language in learning and social contexts which gives information on their 'performance' (i.e. how they use language in the learning environment).
3 Assessment of the language profile may include:
   o speech sound system
   o phonological awareness
   o understanding of language
   o expressive language
   o use of language (pragmatics)
   o understanding and use of figurative language
   o listening and attention skills
   o verbal reasoning skills
   o memory skills
   o voice (quality, volume)
   o prosody
   o fluency
   o non-verbal communication
   o social communication skills.

It is unlikely that all these areas will need to be assessed with any one student.

4  Analysis of the profile.
5  Planning. From the analysis and hypothesis an intervention is planned which is monitored and outcomes evaluated.

The assessment of SLCN is a complex process which is best approached in the context of a multi-disciplinary collaboration. The consensus view of the members of the assessment team will represent a reliable analysis of the needs of the student and avoid the proliferation of labels which some students seem to acquire serially as they move between professionals. This serial approach does no service to the integrity of the assessment process and more 'labels' do not necessarily signify a greater level of educational, social or emotional need.

### Points to remember

- Complex developmental disorders like SLCN require a multi-disciplinary approach to assessment which includes assessment over time and in a range of settings. Without following this approach students may be given inappropriate labels which are hard to revoke at a later stage.
- School staff who have built up a relationship with a student over time and have observed their response to the learning environment and their social interactions with their peers have a key role to play in a multi-disciplinary assessment.

# 10

# Parents Talking

**Chapter Objectives**

> To outline the concerns of parents at transition from primary to secondary school and secondary to further education
> To highlight the problems that students continue to experience at secondary school from a parental perspective
> To use parental experiences to show how different schools have or have not met the needs of students with SLCN
> To present the ongoing concerns that parents have for the future of their children with reference to wider life issues (e.g. independence, friendships, well-being, choice, social communication skills)

The last 20 years has seen increasing opportunities for children with SLCN to receive appropriate specialist support in a mainstream setting in key stages 1 and 2. As more children's needs are seen to be met in the primary sector it is hardly surprising that there is an expectation from parents and professionals that this will be matched when students transfer to secondary school.

## 10.1  Secondary school

There are great differences in the nature and organization of secondary schools compared with those of primary schools:

- The size of the school, buildings are larger, there are more students and staff.
- The scale of the operation is more complex.
- Timetabling is complicated, often on a two-weekly rotation.
- Students need to move around the school from lesson to lesson and arrive at each on time.
- Students need to be able to organize themselves and adjust to interacting with different people, subject areas and methods of working.

- Different equipment will be required for different subjects.
- Homework for a range of subjects needs to be understood, written down, organized, completed and handed in on time.

This complexity, along with the distinctive needs of students with SLCN, and the lack of consistent support at secondary school, causes huge concerns for parents.

## 10.2 What parents said about the system, professionals and inclusion

The proforma for the structured interviews is available on the website.

A sample of mothers was interviewed in order to elicit their opinions and concerns over the way in which their children had been dealt with by the education and health systems. There were 15 students whose ages varied from 12 to 16 years, all but one had received support for their SLCN at primary school and 12 had a Statement of Special Educational Needs. Two students were supported by a specialist facility in their mainstream secondary school.

### 10.2.1 Description of child's SLCN

The first question asked mothers to **describe their child's SLCN.** All had a clear understanding of the nature of their child's difficulties. Some used 'professional' terminology. One mother explained that her child has:

- 'receptive language difficulties – she doesn't always understand what's been said.'
- 'expressive language difficulties – she doesn't always get the words in the right order and her grammar is poor.'
- 'word-finding difficulties – she gets very frustrated.'
- 'dyspraxia – she can't always get the sounds right and sometimes misses out sounds and syllables. She muddles words up like "marshmallow" for "mushroom". She can't organize her language to express her ideas.'
- 'difficulty in recalling instructions – it's her poor auditory memory.'
- 'problems in everyday situations understanding complicated language. She's very literal in her understanding.'
- 'problems learning abstract vocabulary, especially that needed for maths.'

Others used more descriptive language. One mother commented:

'Her complicated verbal skills disguise her language difficulties. For a short while she's okay, but there is no depth to her conversation, it's sort of empty.

She can't think of anything to say – it's called pragmatic difficulties. She can't deal with questions, can't offer an opinion and is always saying the wrong thing and alienating everyone. She really has no idea.'

### 10.2.2 Transition from primary to secondary school

The second question concerned **transition from primary to secondary school**. All parents expressed concern about the level of help that their children would receive at key stage 3 and 4 from both the speech and language therapy service and from the schools. Their concerns are summarized by this parent's comments:

'He started at the language unit and then received help right through junior school. It was brilliant. I got very concerned because there was no guarantee he'd receive the sort of help he'd been getting from everyone and he was moving to this huge school.'

Other concerns were related to wider issues:

- the size of the school
- the size of classes
- teacher awareness of SLCN
- changing classes and teachers
- sharing information about SLCN between teachers
- support available when stressed or anxious
- making friends and being isolated
- vulnerability to bullying
- managing free time.

'His problems are "hidden". It's not like a limp or someone in a wheelchair. He looks like everyone else and I thought they'd find this a problem to understand.'

It is these concerns that were expressed by parents that need to be addressed in the secondary environment.

### 10.2.3 Transition process

The question regarding the actual **transition process** produced mainly favourable comments. The majority of parents were generally satisfied that at least most of the following issues had been addressed:

- Their child was prepared for transition at primary school.
- The SENCO from the secondary school either visited or made contact with the primary SENCO to discuss the child.

- Special arrangements were made on the student visiting day for children to meet key staff such as TAs.
- Alternatively, an extra visit was organized to meet staff, discuss timetables, walk the school, view respite room/areas and so on.

This positive perspective was not shared by one parent who became increasingly concerned when the secondary SENCO expressed the view that the school might not have the appropriate resources and expertise to meet her child's needs.

### 10.2.4 Description of what child enjoyed at secondary school

Parents were next asked to list **what their children enjoyed at secondary school**. For the majority, the responses related to curriculum subjects and 'out of school' activities. Favourite subjects were:

- ICT
- graphic design
- art
- PSHE
- cooking
- sports.

Others were 'out of school' activities such as the Duke of Edinburgh Award, kickboxing or dance club. One distressed parent confided that the only lesson that her son enjoyed was cooking and everything else was 'out of school' activity. Two brothers attending the same school found that the support they gave each other was the most enjoyable aspect of school.

### 10.2.5 Description of what child did not enjoy at secondary school

The parents were next asked about **what their children did not enjoy at school**. 'Maths' was mentioned, as were 'academic subjects', but the question prompted greater concerns about other issues relating to poor speech, language and communication skills:

- 'Relating to other children, socially he finds it very difficult.'
- 'Being bullied. He kept his head down and said nothing but he said he could have killed them, it was awful.'
- 'He wasn't believed by staff, even when it was legitimate.'
- 'He hated the continuous disruption in class by badly behaved children.'
- 'Not being understood by staff.'
- 'Getting into trouble all the time.'

## 10.2.6 Promoting social inclusion

The question on how schools were **promoting social inclusion** evoked mainly negative responses. Only two mothers were fully satisfied with the way the schools actively supported their children. Both schools had special rooms set aside for respite, with staff on duty to monitor break times and sort out difficulties.

Other mothers reported that their children did have access to a named member of staff for when problems arose, but this was seen as 'too little too late'. Several mothers felt extremely stressed by the lack of support for their children. One explained how she felt: 'It drives you mad. I've just given up. All I want is for him to be safe and not get into trouble or be bullied.'

## 10.2.7 Support

All the students received greater or lesser support in class from TAs and some had extra support in a withdrawal special needs area. The majority of mothers expressed the desire for their children to have more support, particularly where a Statement of Special Educational Needs was not in place.

## 10.2.8 Additional help

In response to the next question relating to **additional help**, most mothers wanted more specialist help. Several students were attending a specialist facility and were well supported. A mother of a student not in a special facility said: 'Specialist help would have helped. Helpers (TAs) are ordinary people with no or very little experience of language. Problems need to be sorted out as they arise.'

Another commented:' I'd like someone to come by, a key worker, to see how he is. I want life skills and social communication skills done. Something for self-esteem. The names of these kids are never on the screen for presentations, they feel failures. Why not include them in things they can do like the lighting for drama, so they can achieve something?' A further mother was pleased with what the school had done with extra help for vocabulary and the introduction of icons for homework.

## 10.2.9 Speech and language therapy provision

This question addressed the issue of **speech and language therapy provision**. For students attending a specialist facility, and based in a mainstream class, provision was described as 'brilliant' and 'superb'. 'The therapist works as part of the team, works one to one and with groups as well as advising and supporting teachers in mainstream classes.'

However, for other mothers the picture was not so rosy. Those whose children did not have statements of special educational needs were incensed that therapy was no longer provided because 'they [the children] didn't meet the criteria as from two years ago.' One mother admitted to becoming extremely difficult and confrontational: 'I have become the mother from hell and unbelievably frustrated.'

The remaining mothers were unhappy with levels of provision. One mother commented: 'He had regular therapy through primary school. Now he's seen once in a while.'

## 10.2.10 Specialist teacher service

Those parents who received help from a **specialist teacher service** were pleased with the extra specialist support, but were somewhat perplexed between the disparity of provision between this and the speech and language therapy service. In the area of the survey the specialist teacher visited on a regular basis (not every area will have a specialist teacher service).

## 10.2.11 Greatest concerns

This last question on **greatest concerns** evoked a huge response. The following is a summary of those concerns.

On academic achievement:

- 'Yes, I would like him to achieve, but not to be so pressured, he's never going to be an academic high flyer. I just want him to pursue what he wants and be given lots of options. I'll be worried about him forever. I just want him to have a job and be happy.'

On friendships:

- 'It gets harder as he gets older. I don't want him excluded because he doesn't always understand the teenage "speak" and says the wrong things. I want him accepted and enjoyed for what he is. He's got a friend now and that's good but he'll need help on how to keep a friend and what friendship is all about. Now he's beginning to worry about girlfriends.'

On bullying:

- Two students had experienced bullying so severe that it had extended into the home. One mother said that eggs and stones had been thrown at the house, urination on the front door and verbal and physical abuse of her son. In both cases the police had become involved.

For other mothers, it was an ongoing concern:

- 'They intimidate and harass him to see how he will react, rather than sympathize.'

On inclusion:

- 'I am really concerned about inclusion. It feels like a never-ending battle to get the right support and help.'
- 'I just mentioned that a teacher had not been very understanding and the SENCO was brilliant. She sorted it out in no time.'

On well-being and self-esteem:

- 'As she's got older she's become more aware of her difficulties and worries what other people think about her, that she's stupid. I try to persuade her she's good at lots of things, but I'm not sure it works.'

On independence:

- 'At the moment it feels like they're not capable of being independent. It's agonizing.'

On life skills:

- 'These are so important in fact, almost more important than the rest. At the moment for example he's not even sure he's being rude.'

On any other concerns:

- 'Well what about exams? I'm really concerned. She really struggled and needs more help to understand the questions.'
- 'He continues to have problems with memory and organizational skills and very literal understanding. Even though he's just left school, I have to be there to organize him and explain. I'm really worried that he'll continue to get the right help and support now he's going to FE.'
- 'I really worry about them coping on their own in the future.'
- 'She still relies on me – she's frightened to do things on her own. Sometimes she relies on friends. I'd like her to explain her difficulties,

but she finds explaining hard. Maybe as she matures she'll improve, but I want them to help her with this at school.'

- 'This year they've grouped the children and suddenly he's in the bottom groups for everything. He's totally distraught about it. He's not unintelligent – he has language and social communication problems. I wish I could find another school for him.'
- 'At the moment he doesn't know how to deal with the bullying and not understanding, other than with his fist. He always gets into trouble because of his behaviour and it's his language that's the problem.'
- 'I'd like a speech and language therapist please!'

The views of mothers presented in summary are similar to the concerns expressed in two recent studies by Pratt *et al.* (2006) and Markham and Dean (2006) who found that:

- Provision for young people with speech and language difficulties is very sparse after primary school.
- Difficulties widen with age to include limited NVIQ (non-verbal IQ) and associated behavioural and psychiatric difficulties in adolescence.
- 'Quality of life issues' (e.g. friendships, social communication skills, well-being, independence, choice) become increasingly important to parents as their child matures and more, not less, support is needed.
- There is a lack of awareness by staff and other students at secondary school about the needs of students with SLCN.
- There continues to be great concern about the specific ongoing speech, language and communication needs of their children, but parents now perceive these in a wider 'life' context.

It is of interest that for those mothers whose children were about to enter FE, their concerns continued to be the same. How were their vulnerable children going to be supported and was there anyone with the specialist knowledge available to undertake this task?

In view of the parental comments which echoed the findings of research, schools might like to audit whether they are SLCN friendly. Issues might include:

- What procedures are in place to identify students with SLCN?
- Sharing information with all teachers about the SLCN of students.
- Awareness-raising of SLCN among staff.
- CPD, additional training for staff.
- What modifications are made to the delivery of the National Curriculum? Identify which subject areas make modifications.
- Additional transition planning which includes extra visits, opportunities to meet key staff, practical exercises about getting round the school.
- Special arrangements for free time, if needed.

- A named member of staff for times of stress.
- Support to develop friendships (e.g. Circle of Friends and through the PSHE programmes).
- Support for social skills development.
- Special arrangements for examinations, as needed.
- Promoting life skills and independence skills.
- Partnership with outside agencies; for example, speech and language therapy services (where there is a service).
- Partnership with parents.

Points to remember

- There is a need for both teachers and students to be educated about the nature and needs of students with SLCN.
- The curriculum needs to be differentiated in order to make it and the language used, accessible.
- Specialist support is needed to work with staff in school and resources need to be found to do this successfully.
- Language underpins all learning and subsequent life skills. For these students it needs to be taught as it will not be 'caught'.

# Appendix I: Glossary of Terms

**ADHD:** Attention deficit hyperactive disorder. A neurological disorder characterized by attention difficulties and impulsivity, with or without hyperactivity.

**BICS:** Basic interpersonal communication skills. The early language skills that are acquired in the context of real-life interactions with people that are well established for most children when they enter school.

**CALP:** Cognitive academic language processing. The more abstract and decontextualized demanding language required for learning and accessing the curriculum.

**CATs: Cognitive Assessment Tests:** These are assessments of a range of verbal reasoning skills and used in secondary schools, typically in National Curriculum years 7 and 9.

**Circle of Friends:** A programme designed to help children who have difficulties in making friends. The object is to make sure, through a facilitator, that the child is included in activities at school and feels part of the group.

**Common assessment framework:** A new multidisciplinary framework being gradually introduced for assessing children's needs.

**Conductive hearing loss:** A problem with transmission of sound through the middle or outer ear. Can be improved or cured by medical or surgical treatment.

**CoRT Thinking Programme** (Edward De Bono). The following terms are used:

- CAF: Consider all factors
- PMI: Plus, minus, interesting
- C&S: Consequence and sequel
- AGO: Aims, goals, objective

**CPD:** Continuing professional development. All teachers are expected to improve their skills, knowledge and understanding by further training/study.

**EPS:** Refers to the Educational Psychology Service

**GCSE:** General Certificate of Secondary Education. The name of a set of British qualifications taken by secondary school students at age 14–16 years.

**Key stages:** These refer to the blocks of years into which the National Curriculum is organized. Key stages 1–4 cover ages 5–7 years, 7–11 years, 11–14 years and 14–16 years, respectively. Years 1–11 refer to each year of the National Curriculum.

**National Curriculum (NC):** This sets out the stages and subjects a child will be taught during their time at school. Children aged 5–16 years in 'maintained' or state-funded schools, must be taught the National Curriculum.

**Ofsted:** The official government body for inspecting schools in England, Wales and Northern Ireland.

**Phoneme:** The smallest contrastive unit in the sound system of a language.

**Programmes of study:** For each National Curriculum subject there is a programme of study. These also map out a scale of attainment within the subject. In most key stages 1, 2 and 3 subjects these 'attainment targets' are split into eight levels, plus a level of 'exceptional' performance. These National Curriculum levels give an idea of how a child is progressing compared with what is typical for their age; for example, most children will be at level 4 by the end of key stage 2.

**PRU:** Pupil Referral Unit – specialist educational facility for young people who have BESD who are excluded or otherwise unable to go to school. It provides part time or full time education with the aim of the students returning to full time mainstream education.

**PSHE:** Physical social health education – an area of the curriculum.

**SATs:** Standard Assessment Tests. These are taken by each child at the end of key stages 2 and 3, for Maths, English and Science.

**Sensori-neural hearing loss:** Damage has occurred in the inner ear or there is damage to the auditory nerve and it is permanent although a great deal can be done to reduce its effect (e.g. cochlear implants).

**SENCO:** The Special Educational Needs Co-ordinator. Takes day-to-day responsibility for the operation of the SEN policy and co-ordination of the provision made for individual children with SEN in their school, working closely with staff, parents and carers and other agencies.

**SLCN:** Speech language communication needs. An umbrella term used for children who have significant difficulties with all or several aspects of verbal communication. It is used interchangeably with the terms SLI (specific language impairment) and SLD (specific language disorder).

**Statement of Educational Needs:** Usually called a 'statement', is issued by the Local Authority. They carry out an assessment and make a 'statement', if they decide the help needed by the child cannot be provided from within the school. The 'statement' sets out the child's needs and the help they should have. It is reviewed annually to ensure that any extra support given continues to meet the child's needs.

**Teaching assistant or TA:** Also sometimes referred to as a classroom assistant, learning support assistant (LSA) or individual needs assistant (INA), whose role is to support teachers in school. Duties can vary according to the age of the child/children and include supporting those children with special educational needs.

# References

Afasic Conference April 2007, Bishop, D., Frazier, C., Norbury, J. and Tomblin, B. (eds), *Understanding Developmental Language Disorders in Children,* July 2008.

Aram, et al. (1984) Preschoolers with Language Disorders: 10 years later. *Journal of Speech and Hearing Research,* 17, 232–244.

Argyle, M. (1982) *The contribution of social interaction research to social skills training* in Wine, J.W. and Syme, M.D. (eds), Social Competence, New York: Guildford Press.

Baker, L. and Cantwell, D.P. (1987a) Factors associated with the development of psychiatric illness in children with early speech/Language problems. *Journal of Autism and Developmental Disorders,* 17, 499–510.

Baker, L. and Cantwell, D.P. (1987) A prospective psychiatric follow-up of children with speech and language disorders. *Journal of the American Academy of Child Psychiatry,* 26, 546–553.

Beadle, K.R. (1979) Clinical interactions of verbal language, learning and behaviour. *Journal of Clinical Child Psychology,* 8, 201–205.

Beitchman, J.H. (1985) Therapeutic considerations with the language impaired preschool child. *Canadian Journal of Psychiatry,* 30, 609–613.

Bishop, D. and Adams. (1992) Comprehension problems in children with SLI – literal and inferential meaning. *Journal of Speech and Hearing Research,* 35, 119–129.

Burgess, J. and Bransby, G. (1990) *An evaluation of speech and language skills of children with EBD problems.* College of Speech and Language Therapy Bulletin, 453.

Baird, G. (2007) *Medical Assessment of children with Specific Language Impairment.* AFASIC 4th International Symposium.

Bandura, A. (1969) Influence of model's reinforcement contingencies on the acquisition of imitative responses. *Journal of Personality and Social Psychology,* 1, 589–595.

Barthorpe, T. and Visser, J. (1991) *Differentiation: Your Responsibility.* Tamworth: NASEN.

Bartlett, F.C. (1932) *Remembering.* Cambridge: Cambridge University Press.

Botting, N. and Conti-Ramsden, G. (2000) Social and behavioural difficulties in children with language impairment. *Child Language Teaching and Therapy*, 16, 105–119.

Bradley, P.E. and Bryant, L. (1985) *Children's Reading Problems*. Oxford: Basil Blackwell.

Bristow, J. (1999) *Memory*. London: David Fulton Publishers.

Bryan, K. (2004) A preliminary study of the prevalence of speech and language difficulties in young offenders. *International Journal of Language & Communication Disorders*, 39, 391–400.

Byers-Brown, B. and Edwards, M. (1989) *Developmental Disorders of Language*. London: Whurr Publications.

Camarata, S., Hughes, C. and Ruhl, K. (1988) *Behaviourally disordered students: a population at risk for language disorders*. Language, Speech and Hearing in Schools, Vol. 19, p 191–200.

Cohen, N.J. (1998) Language, achievement and cognitive processing in psychiatrically disturbed children with previously identified and unsuspected language impairments. *Journal of Child Psychology & Psychiatry*, 39, 853–878.

Conti-Ramsden, G. and Botting, N. (1999) Characteristics of children attending language units in England: a national study of 7 year olds. *International Journal of Language & Communication Disorders*, 34, 359–366.

Cotton, K. (1991) *Close-Up #11: Teaching Thinking Skills*. Northwest Regional Education Laboratory's Improvement Research series website: http://www.nwrel.org/scpd/sirs/cu11.html.

Cummins, J. (1986) *Empowering Minority Students: A Framework for Intervention*. Cambridge, MA: Harvard University Press.

Davis, A.D., Sanger, D.D. and Morris-Friehe, M. (1991) Language skills of delinquent and non-delinquent males. *Journal of Communication Disorders*, 3, 14–23.

De Bono, E. (2000) *Six Thinking Hats*. London: Penguin.

De Bono, E. (1995) *CoRT Thinking Programme*. New York: Advanced Practical Thinking.

DfES (1995) Secondary National Strategy. Teaching Speaking and Listening.

Dunn, L.M., Whetton, C. and Burley, J. (1997) *British Picture Vocabulary Scale (BPVS)*. Slough: NFER-Nelson.

Ebbels, S. (2007) Teaching grammar to school-aged children with specific language impairment using shape coding. *Child Language Therapy Teaching*, 23, 62–93.

Freeman, E. and Willig, E. (1995) *Classroom management and instruction for adolescents with language disabilities*. Seminars in Speech and Language, 16, 46–64.

Gerhardt, S. (2004) *Why Love Matters: How Affection Shapes a Baby's Brain*. London: Brunner-Routledge.

Gordon, N. (1991) The relationship between language and behaviour. *Developmental Medicine and Child Neurology*, 33, 86–89.

Goswami, V. (1996) Rhyme and reading. *Child Education*, April 16–17, 2, 124–153.

Gray, C. (1994) *Comic Strip Conversations*. Arlington, TX: Future Horizons.

Hadley, M. and Rice, J. (1991) Predictions of interactional failure in preschool children. *Journal of Speech, Language and Hearing Research*, 34, 1308–1317.

Heneker, S. (2005) Speech & Language Therapy Support for pupils with behavioural, emotional and social difficulties (BESD) – a pilot project. *British Journal of Special Educational*, Vol. 32, No. 2, 2005.

Kerbel, D. and Grunwell, P. (2002) Idioms in the classroom: An investigation of language unit and mainstream teachers' use of idioms. *Child Language Teaching and Therapy*, 2, 114–123.

Lahey, M. and Bloom, L. (1988) 'What is language?' in *Language Disorders and Language Development*. New York: Macmillan, pp. 1–19.

Layton, L., Deeney, K. and Upton, G. (1997) *Sound Practice: Phonological Awareness in the Classroom*. London: David Fulton Publishers.

Leitão, S. and Allan, L. (2003) *Peter and the Cat: Narrative Assessment*. Cowling, Keighley: Black Sheep Press

Locke, A. (1984) *Teaching Talking*. Slough: NFER Nelson.

Mandler, G., Pearlstone, Z. and Koopmans, H.S. (1969) Effects of organisation and semantic similarity on recall and recognition. *Journal of Verbal Learning & Verbal Behaviour*, 8, 410–423.

Markham, C. and Dean, T. (2006) Parents' and professionals' perceptions of quality of life in children with speech and language difficulty. *International Journal of Language & Communication Disorders*, 41, 189–212.

Marshman, A. (1998) *Unpublished Masters Thesis*. University of Birmingham.

Mehrabian, A. (1972) *Non-verbal Communication*. Chicago: Aldine.

Michael McTear and Gina Conti-Ramsden - *Pragmatic Disorders in Children: Assessment and Intervention*. Whurr Publishers 1992.

Mitchell, J. (2003) *A Time to Revise – A Computer Programme*. Surrey: CALSC.

Moats, L.C. and Lyon, G.R. (1993) Learning Disabilities in the USA: Advocacy, Science and the future of the field. *Journal of Learning Disabilities*, 26, 282–294.

Nelson, K. (1981) 'Social cognition in a script framework' in Flavell, J.H. and Ross L. (eds), *Social Cognitive Development: Frontiers and Possible Futures*. New York: Cambridge University Press, pp. 97–118.

Ofsted (1994) *Improving Schools*. London: The Stationery Office.

Passey, J. (1985) *Cued Articulation and Cued Vowels*. Ponteland: Stass Publications.

Pogrow, S. (1988) *Teaching Thinking to At-risk Elementary Students*. Educational Leadership 45/7, pp. 79–85.

Pratt, C., Botting, N. and Conti-Ramsden, G. (2006) The characteristics and concerns of mothers of adolescents with a history of SLI. *Child Language Teaching & Therapy*, 22, 177–196.

Rinaldi, W. (2005) *Language Concepts to Access Learning, LACAL Geography, LACAL Science, LACAL Maths*. Cranleigh: Wendy Rinaldi.

Rupert Technique, Ripley 2006.

Ripley, K (2005). Lecture. Birmingham University, September, 2005.

Ripley, K. and Yuill, N.M. (2005) Patterns of language impairment and behaviour in boys excluded from school. *British Journal of Educational Psychology*, Vol. 75, March 05.

Ripley, K. and Simpson, E. (2007) *First Steps to Emotional Literacy*. Routledge.

Ripley, K., Daines, B. and Barrett, J. (1997) *Dyspraxia: A Guide for Teachers & Parents*. London: David Fulton Publishers.

Ripley, K. Barrett, P. and Fleming, P. (2001) *Inclusion for Children with Speech Impairments – Accessing the Curriculum and Promoting Personal and Social Development*. London: David Fulton Publishers.

Rutter, M. (2007) *Specific Language Impairment and it's Causes: Do we need to change our diagnostic concepts and risk processes*. AFASIC 4th International Symposium.

Snowling, M. and Stackhouse, J. (1996) *Dyslexia, Speech and Language: A Practitioner's Handbook*. London: Whurr.

Spence, S.M. (1995) *Social Skills Training: Enhancing Social Competence with Children & Adolescents*. Slough: NFER/Nelson.

Stackhouse, J. and Wells, B. (1997) *Children's Speech and Literacy Difficulties*. London: Whurr.

Stevenson, J., Richman, N. and Graham, P. (1985) Behaviour problems and language abilities at 3 years and behavioural deviance at 8 years. *Journal of Child Psychology and Psychiatry and Allied Disciplines*, 26, 215–230.

Teasdale, J.D. and Fogarty, S.J. (1979) Differential effects of induced moods on retrieval of pleasant and unpleasant events from episodic memory. *Journal of Abnormal Psychology*, 88, 248–257.

Toomey, M.M. (1994) *Teaching Kids of all Ages and ABC Questions*. Oxford: Winslow Press.

Topping, K. (2001) *Thinking Reading Writing*. Continuum, London and New York.

Vygotsky, L. (1962) *Thought and Language*. Cambridge, MA: MIT Press.

Wallace, B. and Adams, H.B. (1993) *TASC: Thinking Actively in a Social Context*. Oxford: Academic Publishers.

Wang, X., Bernas, R. and Eberhard, P. (2004) *Engaging ADHD Students in tasks with hand gestures: a pedagogical possibility for teachers*. Educational Studies, Vol. 30, No. 3 September 2004.

Warr-Leeper, G., Wright, N. and Mack, A. (1994) Language disabilities of anti-social boys in residential treatment. *Journal of Behavioural Disorders*, 19, 159–169.

# Index

Page numbers followed by f indicate figures; those followed by t indicate tables